On Two Continents: A Long Life's Experience...

Hezekiah Brake

Nabu Public Domain Reprints:

You are holding a reproduction of an original work published before 1923 that is in the public domain in the United States of America, and possibly other countries. You may freely copy and distribute this work as no entity (individual or corporate) has a copyright on the body of the work. This book may contain prior copyright references, and library stamps (as most of these works were scanned from library copies). These have been scanned and retained as part of the historical artifact.

This book may have occasional imperfections such as missing or blurred pages, poor pictures, errant marks, etc. that were either part of the original artifact, or were introduced by the scanning process. We believe this work is culturally important, and despite the imperfections, have elected to bring it back into print as part of our continuing commitment to the preservation of printed works worldwide. We appreciate your understanding of the imperfections in the preservation process, and hope you enjoy this valuable book.

HEZEKIAH BRAKE.

ON TWO CONTINENTS.

A LONG LIFE'S EXPERIENCE.

BY HEZEKIAH BRAKE.

PUBLISHED BY THE AUTHOR.

TOPEKA, KANSAS:
CRANE & COMPANY, PRINTERS.
1896.

HARVARD COLLEGE LIBRARY
BOUGHT FROM THE
AMEY RICHMOND SHELDON
FUND

Entered according to act of Congress, in 1896, in the Librarian's office,
at Washington, by H. BRAKE.

All rights reserved.

THIS BOOK IS DEDICATED

TO THE MEMORY OF

MY WIFE,

WHO SHARED MY JOYS AND SORROWS

FORTY-SEVEN YEARS.

CONTENTS.

CHAPTER.		PAGE.
I.	English Reminiscences	11
II.	Canadian Experiences	41
III.	Eastern Observations	47
IV.	Southern Glimpses	51
V.	Northern Occurrences	55
VI.	Minnesota Pioneering	61
VII.	Missourian Expectations	117
VIII.	A Trip Across the Plains	120
IX.	Life in New Mexico	135
X.	The Return Trip	163
XI.	Life on a Kansas Farm	182
XII.	A Stay in Early Topeka	196
XIII.	Back to the Farm	201
XIV.	Our Experience in Council Grove	228
XV.	Conclusion	238

PREFACE.

The writer has made no attempt in this narrative to portray partisan or political life. The illusory and the dramatic have no place in its pages. It is simply the story of a life through scenes amusing and sorrowful.

The earnest desire of the writer has been to entertain and instruct his fellow-men; to urge upon others the avoidance of the rocks and shoals upon which he has sometimes been wrecked; and to impress the grand lessons of faith, courage, and perseverance, by means of which Providence has enabled him to triumph over obstacles, to secure a competency for his old age, and to find happiness and contentment in the midst of toil and adversity.

If some of the readers of this book shall profit by the lessons taught, and thereby become stronger men and women in the battle of life, the work will have met its reward.

H. B.

INTRODUCTION.

The life of the author of this work has been a remarkable and eventful one. Over eighty years' experience, divided between two continents, has afforded him many opportunities to study the phenomena of nature and human nature.

The opening of paths for the feet of white men, the living among Indians, cowboys and trappers, have often been attended by loss and danger. Travel by night in lonely forests and upon frozen lakes, the building of corduroy roads, the crossing of bogs and floating swamps, narrow escapes from death in the lakes of Minnesota and from the extreme cold of its terrible winters, have fallen to his lot. Crossing the plains in the '50s was attended by many dangers, and to have seen in former times a human being burned alive by Indians did not add to the comforts of the journey. The world owes some recognition to the efforts of pioneers, and few recognize the value of their services or the perils through which they pass in order to make civilization possible.

Within my knowledge, Kansas counties were arid plains, over which roamed the wild Indian and the game he hunted. Later than this, marauders and guerrillas made the State a scene of constant danger, and even civil war penetrated within her borders. But those times are past. The prairies now teem with populous cities, and splendid farms may be found where used to be the Indian hunting-grounds.

As a farmer and stock-raiser, my experience in Kansas may prove useful to some discouraged person, enabling him to work, wait and hope for the success of his undertakings. While as one who has watched the growth of the State, its development from crude beginnings to a symmetry and beauty unsurpassed by other States, it is pleasant to declare that Kansas is in step with the march of civilization, and that the trumpet of progress is for her still sounding — "Onward! Onward!" H. B.

CHAPTER I.

ENGLISH REMINISCENCES.

The old town of Sherborne, Dorset county, England, noted for its ancient abbey and cathedral, was my birthplace. I was born December 4, 1814, and was christened Hezekiah Brake in the Congregational church of my native town, in July, 1815. I was one of a family of nine children — six boys and three girls.

My father was a manufacturer of sail-cloth and linen, and his father lived near us. My grandfather was a poor man, with an enormous family of twenty-two children. Through the benevolence of the Earl of Digby, of the House of Lords, he had been given a piece of land. I never tired of hearing of this great lord, who lived in one of the grandest castles in west England. The great parks, with free and open gates for all comers; the noble swans sporting on the large, beautiful artificial lake; the herd of deer in constant view, and the Earl's magnificent gifts to the poor of town and county, made it seem to me like a tale of fairy-land.

I could not then understand why it was that my grandfather paid, as lord's rent, a half-crown a year. But I afterwards learned that, although a so-called gift, the English law of primogeniture prevented the separation of the land from the home manor.

The eccentricities of my grandfather's influential friend — Earl Digby — greatly interested me. I would have been surprised to be told that the time would come when I would not be interested in the English aristocracy. One instance in particular used to please my childish fancy. A tedious debate had prolonged a session in the House of Lords until the small hours of the night, and the candles (then the means of lighting) needed snuffing. Earl Digby was asleep. Rousing himself from his slumber, he said, "Gentlemen, I have an important remark to make." All was silence. It was the first time the Earl had spoken before the peers. He said:

"Amputate the redundancy of those superfluous luminaries."

The Earl was a great friend to the High Church of England. In those days dissenters were pointed out with scorn, and "Methodist" was a term of opprobrium. Feeling ran high against those who had received favors from the Church of England and had afterwards adopted other doctrines of religion. Especially severe was the verdict if, as in my grandfather's case, John Wesley's doctrines were favored. As a consequence, my grandfather and his large family were reduced to poverty. My father brought him home to live with us until his death.

I have space for but few incidents of my childhood, but the demonstrations made each 5th of November left an impression upon my boyish mind too lasting to pass by without mention. When I was ten years old, I participated in one of those occurrences. I did not know then why we rolled tar-barrels to augment the blaze of the huge bonfire. I supposed it was to have a jolly time. But I learned afterwards that it was to celebrate a day of thanksgiving, not only for deliverance from the Guy Fawkes conspiracy, but for the perpetuation of the Protestant religion.

It seemed a horrible thing to me when I heard that Fawkes and his conspirators had once provided thirty-six barrels of gunpowder for explosion, in order to destroy the official leaders of Great Britain.

Between the ages of seven and fourteen I attended the abbey school. At the latter age I left school to assist my father in his business. About this time, linen products woven at home were superseded by cotton fabrics made by machinery. After struggling three years against the misfortunes brought upon him by the new inventions, my father left his family and went to America.

After the first shock of my father's desertion was over, I rallied my courage and secured a position, three miles from my home, at Milborne Port, in the counting-house of a Methodist class-leader and preacher, Reverend Edward Ensor. Through his encouragement, I taught in the Sunday school for several months, but the first serious impressions of religion experienced by myself were received from a local preacher named Cox, at Stone Chapel, Milborne Port, Somerset. The thought upon which the sermon was based was a warning to young men. "While he was trifling about many things," the minister said, "death came and life departed."

Fearing to trifle longer, I joined the Methodist church. I was only twenty years of age, but was put on the circuit as an exhorter. I shall never forget the audacity of the elder who sent me to preach in some of the new chapels. I remember some of the people cried when I talked to them. I hope they did not forget the lessons taught.

I soon realized my lack of fitness for a Bible teacher, and began to better qualify myself for the sacred work. On my knees until after midnight, I might often have been found studying for the ministry. Doctor Dwight's "System of Theology," Doctor Paley's "Difficulties of Infidelity," and Baxter's "Commentary," were the most important books in my possession. Perhaps the greatest aid I received in preparing to cope with infidelity and teach theology was from my actual work as teacher in the Methodist Sunday school at Milborne Port. My class was composed of six boys between the ages of sixteen and twenty-one. Not one of them knew a letter of the English alphabet. But in a year they had learned to read pretty well, and soon after they became members of the church.

Milborne Port was at that time a borough town. It was not an uncommon sight to see the fighting factions engaged in rivaling each other in securing votes. When the members of the Parliament came down, fifty-pound cheeses, huge loaves of bread and great barrels of beer were rolled out among the writhing, struggling masses of voters. Thousands of pounds sterling were often spent in this little town by the aspirants for Parliamentary honors. Milborne Port was a dilapidated-looking place, several hundreds of years old. Railroads have since improved it, but at that time there were none in existence. Its chief feature was a glove factory, which employed many persons of both sexes from the adjoining country. My duties were to examine the sewing of the women and girls, and to help pack the gloves for the London market.

The time spent here passed pleasantly. I had taken up my residence with the family of a Mr. Hobbs. His daughter, Miss Harriet, was a fellow-teacher with me in the Sunday school. I fell violently in love, and became engaged to her. Arrangements were made for a speedy marriage.

Full of pleasing anticipations of the wedding-day, I made a trip to Bath for some necessary housekeeping purchases. Upon my return at night, I was refused admission. Surprised beyond measure, I inquired upon what grounds, and was informed that Mr. Hobbs, who was ailing, had died suddenly that day. Before expiring, he had made a dying request of his daughter, which she had promised to grant. The promise was to the effect that she should remain unmarried, and devote her life to her mother.

The blow fell upon me with crushing weight. With all the money I had with me spent except a single sixpence, even my wedding clothes in the house of the woman who had jilted me, in a fit of temporary insanity I turned away from occupation, friends, home and religion, and set my face toward London.

I remember that I dreamed I was sleeping on a bed of straw that night. When morning dawned, sore with disappointment, I started on foot for the metropolis. It was in the spring of 1836. There were no railroads in that part of England, so I could not walk on the ties, and I had no money to go by coach. There was nothing to be done but follow the hot, dusty road, and I wearily plodded on without stopping to think what I should do when I reached my destination. About midway, I paid fourpence for a bed and twopence for bread. As I dared not beg for fear of being arrested for vagrancy, during the rest of the way I ate Swede turnips for food. It was not until the close of the second day that I finished the long journey of one hundred and ten miles.

In spite of my thick-soled, hob-nailed shoes, the flinty roads blistered my feet, and during the latter part of the journey, I suffered more than I can describe.

Providence conducted me safely to my good uncle, James Hyde, then a resident of London. His wife, my father's sister, gave me an affectionate welcome, and I was employed in my uncle's livery business.

My new home was at the foot of Westminster Bridge, on the Lambeth side. My uncle had many horses, cabs and carriages for hire, and was a proficient veterinarian and horse-trainer. He promised to teach me how to make an honest living, and to bear with my inexperience until I had mastered my profession.

I borrowed a pound sterling and sent it in a letter to my mother. After acquainting her with the particulars of the matter, I asked her to collect my books and clothing, and send them to me in London. My other property I desired her to give to my false sweetheart. She did as I requested. I never saw my love again; neither did I ever return to the work of the ministry.

After a time, I received the following letter from my mother:

"SHERBORNE, DORSET, April 15, 1836.

"*My Dear Son:* You are now of the age of about 21 years and 4 months, and have been frightened off from your home, your employment, and I am afraid from your religion, your services in the Sabbath school, and apparently from all your friends. From what I can learn, your sweetheart's parents — through the death of her father and his request — have shut you out of house and home although so near your matrimonial alliance. There may be some reasonable allowance for them and some providential fatuity toward yourself. You have my dearest sympathy. As you have safely footed it to your uncle's home in London, and as your aunt Mary Hyde, your poor father's sister, knows that he has gone off to America, perhaps never to return, and has left me with your brothers and sisters to care and provide for, she will surely see you well done by.

Your Uncle Hyde is a good and capable man, so I advise you to work well for him, maintain your good character, and you will insure confidence, without which no one in human life can succeed. I thank you much for your consideration in getting and sending me the 20 shillings. Very necessary to have your things got together; it is a large box, and contains what you desired; the furniture is given as you directed, to your Harriet, with your prayers for all that is good for her and her family. I hope you will safely receive the box. Write me as soon as possible. I am as well as can be expected with all my great troubles. From your ever-loving mother until death, SARAH BRAKE."

I now found myself installed in a position, the duties of which I knew but little, but I was willing to work and do my best at whatever was given me to perform. I worked at keeping accounts, and also learned to groom, ride and drive horses. It was customary then as now to tip courteous grooms, and the shillings thus received eked out my low wages. The people about me were rough, and my surroundings poorly accorded with my past experience. But I made the best of circumstances, and treated the scorn of my companions with silence.

My uncle's family, besides himself and wife, consisted of two boys — William and Duke — (the latter was named for the Duke of Wellington), fourteen and eighteen years of age, neither of whom was a Christian. All of the sweet and hallowed influences of my peaceful country life had been rudely swept aside. I now found myself surrounded with employés who never entered church or Sabbath school, and who seemed ignorant of the commandments issued amidst the thunderings of Sinai.

I tried, however, to stand by my faith, and at first succeeded. I remember at this time attending a great ministerial association in London. Exeter Hall was full of learned ministers of the gospel. The remarks of a gentleman from Scotland especially interested me. He said:

"We have come here by many roads—from the north, the south, the east, the west. Many of the roads traveled have been full of inequalities and stumbling-blocks. Nevertheless we are here. We have arrived at the great metropolis in safety. Hushed be our differences. Let our highest object be to gain that higher metropolis for which we are all striving. Let us quarrel no more over doctrines. Our Redeemer never quarreled."

At that time, I was greatly concerned over my danger of falling away from religious teaching, and I thought the gentleman's speech most excellent, as it helped me to understand that one could be a Christian and belong to any denomination.

Aside from my uncouth companions, the novelty of life in the greatest city of the world enticed me often into forgetfulness of all but the enjoyment of pleasure. Situated as I was, near Westminster Bridge, the ruins of the burned-down Parliament buildings were in sight, and the workmen were busy driving piles for the erection of the present edifice.

Among other sights then of interest in London was the Polytechnical Institute, where I laughed at Madame Tussaud's wax-work figures, and climbed into the carriage occupied by Napoleon the day he was captured by the English general.

The British Museum did not interest me so much as the Tower of London, that memorial of the cruelties of bygone generations when the axe was considered the cure for political offenses. The great amphitheater was opposite our stables. The famous horse, Mazeppa, which, although thirty years old, used to lie down at the close of the performances as the curtain fell, was a prime favorite of mine. Being so near the great theater, I attended the plays very often. I well remember the night the building caught fire. Having risen early to attend to my duties in the stable, I first saw the flames. I ran into the adjoining houses and roused the still sleeping people. When the street was full of scantily-clad persons, and the danger to life was over, I looked at the progress of the fire; as I did so, the great chandelier presented to the theater by George IV. fell into the pit with a terrible crash.

I was one of the vast concourse of sight-seers in Westminster Abbey when Victoria was crowned Queen of the United Kingdom. A mighty throng had pushed me along until the coronation was over and the crowd had surged out of the building. When I escaped, I had lost a shoe and stocking, and had to walk home across Westminster Bridge half barefooted.

The Queen's Horse Guards at the Admiralty were of great interest to me. One never tired of watching those fine six-foot-tall fellows in their splendid uniforms. But the scenes connected with the wedding of Queen Victoria left the most vivid impression on my mind. A magnificent review of the Queen's troops was held in the St. James Park. After this the whole city was splendidly illuminated in honor of the occasion.

In my journey up the Strand, through Temple Bar, and on through the old city, I lost my cousins. I was so weary that I fell asleep on a doorstep, and was taken into custody by a policeman. He took me off, I think to Bow Street station, but in the morning, pitying my rural innocence, and sharing my sympathy in the Queen's marriage, released me from custody. My own disappointment in wedlock came over me afresh. I actually envied the Queen, as if she could help my having borne misfortune, and never felt myself even with her until I came to America and was naturalized.

Meanwhile, my studies in horsemanship progressed rapidly. The first time I rode horseback my uncle started me upon a partly-broken sorrel mare down Belvidere road to the foot of Waterloo road, by way of Rowland Hill Chapel. The mare ran into a livery yard, and some men then drove her out, after which I could not hold her. I started her homeward, but she ran into an apple-cart and upset an old woman's prospects for apple-selling. The woman yelled, "Police!" I broke into a cold sweat as I hurried the refractory brute homeward. In my haste to cross the bridge, I ran over a woman and knocked her down, and the mare went on and into the stables. Soon after an officer appeared with a summons, and I had to go with him. My jolly uncle paid my fine of sixteen shillings for "fast riding across a sidewalk," and for several days my experience as a rider furnished fun for the whole force of employés about the yard.

My uncle's knowledge of veterinary skill was cheerfully imparted to me, and the information he gave me has often proved invaluable. He was a kind-hearted man, but his acquaintance with turf sportsmen often led him to liquor-drinking. He would then try to remove my verdancy by satirical conversation. He little knew that —

"Satire, like a polished razor keen,
Wounds with a touch scarcely felt or seen."

I tried, however, to bear it patiently, and to do all I could to repay his kindness, as well as that of my good aunt, who was like a mother to me. Her death shortly after is still a sorrowful memory in my mind.

I soon learned to ride, drive cabs and carriages, and was often sent to take ladies and gentlemen through the metropolis. These persons were usually members of the aristocracy residing in London, and were often cruel to the persons serving them. An incident that occurred during my service with my uncle will illustrate my meaning. "Frank," one of our coachmen, came home early one morning nearly blind, and too faint to walk. As I helped him into my counting-room, I said:

"I suppose you are drunk."

"No," he replied, "but I had a fight coming home with the Marquis of Waterford."

I found his statement to be true. The previous evening, Frank had taken the Marquis to Richmond, and remained with the horses while that gentleman entered a baker's shop.

In those times, bakers kept their flour in large three-hundred-pound sacks in the shops, where it could be seen. The Marquis had seized the baker's wife, and thrust her head into one of these sacks of flour. The baker being near, the Marquis jumped into the carriage, and threw the coachman a guinea to induce him to drive more rapidly. Frank did his best, but the man beat him to make him drive faster. The next day the baker, who had learned the name of the rascally Marquis, made his appearance in court, and with Frank swore to the facts in the case. A little gold, however, released the defendant. It would not be so easy to evade the law now as it was then. Money has less power to-day in Great Britain to protect the rich in trampling down the poor than it possessed sixty years ago. From the example of the good Queen, English aristocracy has learned many important lessons.

After remaining with my uncle over two years, I persuaded him to seek for me a different situation. He consented, and secured me a position with a gentleman who kept thoroughbred hunting-horses. The duties of my position consisted in grooming the horses, and following my employer after the hounds in the proper season. Lord L.'s town house was in London, his county house in Surrey, near the town of Guildford. I followed him from one place to the other with the horses.

The latter were fine animals, named "General" and "Rough Robbin." I dressed them day and night, a suitable dress being provided for the purpose. The night dress was an all-wool blanket, with breast, face and neckhood trimmed in scarlet and a well-fitted back-line and surcingle. The day dress was of the same pattern, but made of fine, well-trimmed linen. Nicely braided mats of straw were spread in the clean, airy stable, beside the noble horses.

Lord L. was afraid of "Robbin," and it was part of my work to break the high-strung creature. I soon taught the horse to scale ditches, fences, hedges, and wicket gates. In one of these breaking expeditions, as we scaled a high wicket, I lost my hat and was obliged to go home with a kerchief on my head. This so delighted his lordship that I was at once fairly installed in my new position.

About this time, my two sisters Priscilla and Athaliah and my brother Philip came to London, and paid me a visit. Obtaining good situations, they remained, and my sisters afterwards married in the city. One of them introduced me to a friend of hers, a beautiful young lady to whom I paid court for over a year. For the second time in my life I became engaged. Too poor to marry, it was some time, even with the most careful economy, before I could save enough to make preparations for our wedding. When at last my circumstances would admit of marriage, I went to Clapham Common, where she resided, to see my destined bride. To my poignant sorrow, I learned that she was dead, and that two days previous her corpse had been placed in the old cemetery of Whitechapel. I am incapable of drawing on my imagination, but as I remember the anguish I suffered at not even seeing her dead face, after more than fifty years my eyes are full of tears.

I was now ordered down to Surrey to prepare the horses for the chase. Aside from sweating and grooming both of them, I had to especially exercise "General." He had killed his previous groom, and was a dangerous horse. A little way from Guildford is a low range of hills; they were then called "the Hog's Back." This was the starting-point of the chase, and from here to Farnborough was a run of seven miles. From the Hog's Back, I started "General." I tried as we neared the turnpike to stop him, but failed in the attempt. Before the keeper could open the gate, the horse overleaped it. I braced myself and stopped him on the other side of the gate, but in so doing sprung a bone in my wrist which has ever since projected — a mark of the labor required by sporting-men of their grooms.

After a few days, I saw my first chase. The quarry was a stag provided by the sportsmen for the purpose, and this was to be followed by a chase with fox and harrier hounds. On the morning of the hunt all was excitement. Horns of strong beer were emptied, the stag-hounds were held in readiness and the noble stag turned loose. Fiery horses ridden by both ladies and gentlemen dashed away in pursuit, eager to be first to close in on the game. Lamed horses fell behind, and thrown riders, splashed with mud, lay and sat lamenting. Many of the actors in the scene covered more than fifty miles that day, over ditches, fences, and hedges.

When, amidst dirt, fatigue and clamor the chase ended, I took my horses and went home, tired and disgusted with the whole miserable, wicked performance. I was not long in reaching the conclusion that no Christian gentleman would have assisted in such utter disregard for life and property, and resolved to quit my employer as soon as possible. That night as I dressed the jaded horses, I thought sadly of the poor farmers whose crops were damaged by the day's work, and wondered how the winning of a chase after the Queen's stag could reconcile these people to the loss of crowns of gold in the hereafter. When the chase for the hares and bold Reynard was over, and a new groom secured, I quitted Lord L.'s service and walked back to London.

I went into lodgings the next day. My uncle had moved away, and I had no friends. I began at once to look for a situation, and soon secured one in the Strand near St. Clement's church as coachman. Doctor James Scott, inventor of the stomach pump and many other medical instruments, was my employer. His family consisted of himself, wife, and their son, Montague — since an eminent lawyer.

As I had no care of the horses, (they being kept at livery,) I filled the place of a general attendant in the family at home, and also attended Lady Scott as coachman. She was fond of riding, and praised or scolded me beyond measure in accordance with my securing or failing to secure for her the precedence in entrance at bazaars or museums over other dignitaries. She also took great pains in teaching me how to become a proficient waiter. I filled up the odd moments polishing silver, beating carpets, and traveling over the city, often until midnight, delivering medical instruments at the homes of sick persons. When I had a leisure hour, humbly trying in the midst of all this multiplicity of services to work at character-building, I secured tickets to the Lord Chancellor's law lectures in Temple Bar. Dickens has immortalized this street. Its gardens, its lawyers, its bewigged and gowned Chancellor will never lose their interest to his readers.

After six months, native restlessness or some other influence caused me to quit the Doctor's service, and seek elsewhere what might be in store for me by Providence.

Passing along Regent street, well dressed and newly shaved — for although looking for work it was like a holiday to me — I heard my name called by an unknown cabman. The man was ragged, poor and forlorn-looking. As I neared him, to my surprise I recognized my cousin of the stables near Westminster Bridge — William Hyde. He told me that Duke had died of disease brought on by drunkenness. His father, too, after failing in business, had died a victim to the drink habit. As I looked at poor William, I saw that he was also following in the footsteps of his father and brother.

"Well," he said, "what are you doing?"

"Walking the streets," I replied, "looking for work."

"Where's your kit?" he asked.

"In a small room in Drury Lane," I said.

"I am married," said William, "and have two rooms

in Standgate street over the bridge, Lambeth side. Let me get your things, and you go with me. This is my cab, and it is all I have to depend upon for my living."

He got my box, and took me to his home, and I stayed with him a week. His wife was a pleasant person, but such poverty on every hand I have seldom seen. I felt myself an intruder upon their distress, and most eagerly sought a situation. Hearing of one in Tavistock Square, I applied for it, and was admitted into a spacious drawing-room where I answered the many questions put by the lady of the house.

"Your character is all right," she said, in conclusion, "but I am afraid you are not tall enough. It takes height and length of arms to handle dishes, but please walk down this long room and I will see."

Chagrined at her request, I walked down the room and through the door, and the butler laughed as he let me out into the Square. Once outside, I blamed myself for taking offense and perhaps losing a situation because the lady had unduly criticized my proportions, and I resolved that another such scene should not occur. With renewed diligence I set to work, and after reading numerous advertisements, and applying at different intelligence offices, I at last learned of a vacant place in the family of Nathaniel Gould, Tavistock Square, near Old Oxford street, where I was fortunate enough to make an engagement.

Mr. Gould was a lumber dealer, who transported the products of Canadian forests to London; he had received many handsome silver souvenirs for his success in the work. He was much engrossed with his business, which received his attention at Barge Yard, Bucklersbury, in the heart of the old city, and the family kept as few servants as possible. For this reason, I wore a footman's livery at home and a coachman's livery abroad. It left me little idle time, and gave me much hard work, but my stay in Standgate street had lightened my purse, and I was very glad to have the situation.

On Sundays, carrying the prayer-book, and dressed in a richly-trimmed suit with big, silver buttons, I walked behind the family of eight persons to church. On weekdays, when not otherwise engaged at home, I drove the fat black horses with the family in the carriage. The horses were rat-tailed, and wore false tails which swept the ground. I shudder to think what Mrs. Gould would have said if one of those showy horse-tails had come off at some fashionable gathering. Sometimes Mr. Gould would spend the Sabbath in driving his family to some suburb of the city, and then only was I free to seek amusement with my friends.

St. John's Wood, Norwood, Chalk Farm and Blackheath were favorite places of resort for Londoners in 1842. As coachman, I of course had an opportunity to visit all of these places, but it was when I was ordered to follow the family to Brighton with the carriage and horses, and I knew we were really going to the seaside, that I received my first great pleasure in this service.

As usual in those times, the family traveled by stages with four horses and two postilions, the latter wearing jockey caps, leather breeches and top boots. Following Mr. Gould's instructions to the letter, I reached Brighton in safety with my part of the charge. This popular place of resort was then considered the best of English watering-places, and rents were very high. Mrs. Gould paid five hundred pounds sterling for the use of a mansion for three months.

The change from the turmoil of London to the refreshing breezes of the quiet sea was greatly enjoyed by each member of our large party, and by none more so than by myself. The time sped all too swiftly for our return, but at last "Bobby" and "Double" were hitched to the carriage, and as on the way down, the family started by stage with postilion, while I took the team home.

Midway to London, I stopped at the Crawley Hotel for the night, and while asleep a thief entered my room, relieved me of all my money, and left me to pawn my watch for my board bill. I was half starved when at last I reached London.

Mr. Gould's family often gave princely dinners, and as he was a very popular gentleman, and gathered a fine class of people about him, I found their conversation, which my duty as footman often compelled me to overhear, a source of education to me, and I tried to use it for my self-improvement.

I soon grew tired of this place, and gave notice that I must leave Tavistock Square. The old coachman came back, and I quitted my employer with paid-up wages, glad to be free from such servitude.

My sisters were still in London, and I spent a short time in showing them about the city. As I had left my best suit of private clothes with my cousin, William Hyde, when I went to Brighton, I now took a cab and went after my property. To my sorrow, when I reached the place I learned that my poor friend had fallen a victim to his appetite for drink. He had gone to that "bourne from whence no traveler returns." His helpless widow, in the lowest depth of poverty and ill-health, had been obliged to see her sick babe die of sheer want. Once a beautiful brunette with lovely features and large, dark eyes, now with eyes sunken and cheeks pallid, she was the picture of sorrow and despair. My clothing had been pawned, then her furniture sold to help sustain life in her dying child. Drunkenness — the fiend — had triumphed after all her feeble efforts, and as usual, had led his victims through scenes of disease, misery and death.

Dear reader, did you ever witness the sorrow of a beloved, innocent relative too late to be of assistance? If so, as your lips trembled and your heart thrilled with sympathy until floods of tears relieved your overcharged heart, you experienced some of my feelings as I looked at poor Mrs. Hyde.

This occurred about the time of Father Matthew's demonstration against strong drink. The vast concourse of people, the great parade, and the numerous banners, to me are connected vividly with my cousin's death. One inscription read:

"We would rather eat it."

The banner displayed below the words a huge loaf of bread. The demonstration did much good. Many of the best families ceased to give beer and gave tea instead to their employés. But the temperance agitation came too late to save my cousin.

I found my clothes in a pawnshop at Mid street, Covent Garden, and redeemed them for a sovereign.

After a short time spent in visiting my sister, I secured a place at number 23 Hyde Park Square, as a liveried footman. Behold me now in a white pigeon-tailed coat with black velvet collar adorned with silver lace, black plush knee breeches, and long white stockings. Thankful for the change from Tavistock Square, I remained in this situation two years.

The family was a very religious one, and attended the nearest Episcopal church. The old cathedral and abbey at Sherborne were Episcopal institutions, and it was a pleasure to me to follow the familiar religious service. The master's name was Sir John H. Beckles.

Much has been said of wealth and intelligence against poverty and ignorance, in regard to employers and employés, but I never felt that I had forfeited my independence in becoming a serving-man. Although as a non-property-holder, I had no vote, and therefore no voice in the government of my country, I realized that all enterprises had drawbacks, and that service at least had few responsibilities, and instead of complaining, I set to work to save my earnings. I soon began to lay by some money towards rising, as I afterwards did, to independence.

In the summer of 1843, I accompanied the family to St. Leonard's on the sea. We traveled, as was then the custom, by coach, with postilion and two spans of horses. Making ten-mile stages at a time, we soon reached the resort in safety. The journey was made in style, the coachman following with the carriage for the use of the family. A splendidly furnished mansion was taken, and occupied upon their arrival by the family and servants.

The sea of course was the chief attraction, but the town of Hastings near by was often visited. Its beautiful hop gardens were then in full bloom, but the greatest pleasure we enjoyed was a visit to the home of the great astronomer, Herschel. The place was called Hearse Green, and overlooked the sea. The sun-dial and the large telescope were features long remembered.

The return home was performed in the same way we had gone to St. Leonard's. More or less danger attended the ancient way of traveling. Haste and speed were always demanded, the driver being expected to make ten or twelve miles an hour. Wheels, horses, even the postilions often gave trouble and caused delay. It was the custom to allow the men liquor on the way home, and few refused the brandy and water offered in intended generosity. Temperate principles among servants were seriously endangered at these public houses on the way to and from London.

The next expedition to the country was made for the health of the baby of the family, and was to the Malvern Hills. From here the beautiful city of Worcester was in full view, and the bracing atmosphere of the hills was delightful. Myself and the maid attendants accompanied Lady H. Beckles. A female donkey, milked twice a day in the kitchen, provided milk for the sick child. "Jennie" became such a friend of mine that she often followed me down to the postoffice. The recovery of the child being accomplished, we returned to the city.

The real arrangements for the summer were now made. We went to visit the spa waters at Cheltenham. A railroad had been constructed to that town, and for the first time we all went on the cars to our destination. The charming walks and drives, as well as the healthful spa waters at this lovely place, made the three months of our sojourn pass all too quickly.

The inevitable return to London was hardly completed until the usual round of balls, shopping and visiting began. Then, as now, fashionable people spent the whole round of existence in an unending, fruitless pursuit after the unattainable in this world — perfect happiness.

But to me the balls given and attended were very amusing. At one of these, as the weather was damp, rolls of matting were stretched from the entrance to the carriage-way. Link-men holding lights called the carriages, about fifty of which were in waiting for the guests, and the ladies walked to them dryshod on the matting.

Lady H. Beckles was a true lady, and always treated me with the utmost kindness and respect. In her home, visitors always appeared before ten o'clock. Elegantly attired in livery, wearing white gloves, it was my duty to usher into her presence the callers, or to present upon a silver waiter the cards or letters received. At two in the afternoon, the carriage was called and the family driven about for the daily ride. We usually drove in Rotten Row, where the most elegant equipages were daily seen.

A dinner in those days was a very elaborate affair, and one given over fifty years ago may interest my readers. At this dinner, served to a select party of twelve friends, I performed the duties of butler, and overhauled the plate, under my care in the pantry adjoining my bedroom, for use at the dinner. It consisted of a vast quantity of both gold and silver plate, heirlooms of two old families. To clean and polish enough for the occasion required the most of three days and nights. All of the plate bore the family crest — the "hand and dagger." The order consisted of four dozen solid silver forks, four dozen silver steel knives, (silver knives being then made so dull, they were a little worse nuisance than at present, and were not used,) five dozen spoons, large and small, and one dozen handsome silver napkin-rings. There was also to be a great epergne for the center of the table, flanked by large, beautiful vases; the latter were for ices and rare old wines. Two of the corners of the long table were furnished with eight large covered dishes, with many larger covers for the heavier viands. Two immense chandeliers with six silver branches for the reception of the large wax candles which lighted the table, were suspended over it; another of the same description hung over the sideboard in the dining-room. A twenty-pound solid silver salver ornamented this sideboard, with a smaller one either side of this monster of a center-piece.

The caterer and waiters came from Oxford street. The following bill of fare prepared by him was served at the dinner:

FIRST COURSE.
Soups.
Soup Italienne.   Mock Turtle.
Fish.
Cod Head, Baked.   Fillets of Soles.
Entrees.
Suprene of Fowls.   Mutton Cutlets.
Oyster Patties.   Fillets of Woodcock.

SECOND COURSE.
Roasts.
Roast Beef.   Roast Hare.
Removes.
Briocke and Pamison Cheese.   Souffle of Chocolate.
Entreements.
Mushrooms a la Provençale.   Scalloped Oysters.

DESSERT.
German Apples.   Jellies.
Tarts.   Candied Grapes.

A few days after this dinner, my sister Priscilla came with my mother to visit me. I had not seen the latter for several years, and in my eagerness to see her I went out to the carriage in my livery. My sister pointed me out to her. To my great chagrin, I heard my mother say:

"There goes a fine popinjay."

She had never known the humiliation attached to such service.

My mother was hardly gone when Sir John received word that he had lost a lot of slaves in Demarara. They had been emancipated and his plantation was ruined. Knowing that he was obliged to make some retrenchments, and fearing that I was one of the persons with whose service he might dispense, I gave warning and soon after quitted the situation. Not in the least discouraged at being out of employment, I set to work and soon found a place as footman in a family consisting of an old gentleman over eighty years of age, and a lady. They resided in Mayfair near Park Lane, and as the butler gave most of his time to his master, Mr. E., a great deal of heavy work fell upon my shoulders.

Mr. E. was a very eccentric character. He had been a great London barrister, whose efforts had been crowned with success, but he was now an avowed infidel. Although generous to his servants, he was very hard to please. Something of a philosopher, he insisted that a man might live to the age of Methusaleh if he did not have to bear with a set of fools who would not lower the top-sashes in his room and let out the carbon *di-oxide*. Five days out of seven he would order the carriage and drive in the park or go to St. James's Club House. The lady went in the carriage with him in the park, and as footman I had to stand up at the back, exhibiting my black-and-white livery in all sorts of weather.

Sometimes Mr. E. attended a ball, and the coachman

and myself waited outside for his return. It was customary, in order to shorten the time, for the waiting-men to go off to the nearest gin palace after a pot of porter. One night the coachman drove off for this purpose, with several others of his class, and while gone the link-men, whose duty it was to do so, called the carriage. Mr. E. took a cab and went home. Upon our return, frightened nearly to death at the certainty of our discharge, we hurried after him. On entering the house the butler said:

"I tell you, Brake, you had better go up to his room."

I went, trembling at the thought of the old gentleman's wrath over being obliged to call a cab while his coachman and footman rode in his carriage, up the stairs and knocked at his door.

"Come in!" he thundered.

I went in, bowing and apologizing.

"Go away to bed!" he shouted. "Don't I know that you cared nothing about me and went to sleep in the carriage? I could not expect anything else of two ignoramuses."

I went down-stairs, leaving Mr. E. shouting for the butler to come and open his windows, and that was the last I heard of the matter.

Lord and Lady Lennigan, of Fogerty Castle, Ireland, came to visit Mr. E., who was Lady L.'s father, and soon after Clifton Heights were selected as the attraction for the summer. The pretty little town of Clifton, in Gloucestershire, on the banks of the River Severn, and near to Bath — the cleanest city in England — was a most delightfully healthy place. We found much here to interest us. A basket upon ropes suspended from height to height formed a unique ferry by which passengers crossed the river. Strolling along the green banks of the Severn, we once saw the prototype of Dickens's *Fat Boy* lying on the grass.

"What makes you so fat?" asked Mr. E.

"Not eating and drinking, sir," replied the fat boy.

"What then?" asked Mr. E.

"Happiness and contentment," was the reply.

Mr. E. gave him a shilling for his wit, and the lazy rascal did not even get up to thank him.

Once we met a schoolmaster with about fifty pupils, on some botanical excursion. The old gentleman asked him what he taught them. The schoolmaster replied:

"I teach them not only the letter of the Word, but the spirit and meaning thereof."

"Teach them above everything to have common-sense," growled my irascible employer.

After awhile I grew tired of constant attendance upon an infidel, and resolved to seek service with more religious people. I was fortunate enough soon after to secure a situation with a wealthy Christian family. Providence must have guided me, for, listening to reading and prayers twice a day not only helped me to shake off the irreligious influences of my past home, but here I met a lovely young woman, refined and gentle, who at this time was a domestic in the family of my new employer. Aside from her native graces, she was an adept in the art of cookery, having studied under Francatelli, Queen Victoria's serving-man. The family held Charlotte in the highest esteem. She was, though poor, of a good old English family. Her father was a quaint but sturdy Englishman, and her only sister was the wife of Lord Crump. After the lapse of many years, again I fell in love — this time with Charlotte

Cranham, the cook, and at last the course of true love ran smoothly. I now resolved to retain this situation until by careful economy I could save enough money to enable me to marry and cross the ocean in search of a home in free America.

Spring came, and the usual annual trip to Hastings was made by the B. family. Our party was a large one. There were six of the family, two maids, and myself. We traveled in two coaches with four span of horses. On the way down an accident occurred: the horses gave out. We were fortunate enough to find an omnibus in the village where we halted; I procured four fresh horses, and again we started. We had gone only a few miles when one of the wheels burst into a blaze. I was obliged to put the family out of the carriage and get another wheel before we could proceed on our journey.

From Hastings I wrote my first letter to Charlotte, who had been left behind to keep house. As she fancied soles, and this was a great place for them, I procured a basketful and sent them to her. Of course she had to write and thank me for the fish, and also send good wishes for my safe home-coming.

Upon our return to the city, I told the B. family that my mother, who still resided in Sherborne, wished to see me, as she had heard from one of my sisters in London that I was going to America. I also stated that I must leave their service, which I did a week later. Leaving my effects in the care of my sweetheart, I took the train for Southampton, and from there walked across to my native home.

After our greetings were over, I told my mother that I

thought of marriage, but was not sure I liked the idea of a speedy wedding. She replied:

"Why, my son, you are old enough to marry; you will be thirty-two in two months — on the fourth of December. You have been single too long. When I know you are settled I shall feel more comfortable about you."

That decided the matter. I resolved to marry upon my return to London.

I spent a week in Dorset county. While there, as I was on the way home from visiting some old acquaintances, a big fellow accosted me:

"Well, Hezekiah, do you know me?"

"No," I answered.

"I am Jacob Bugler," he answered; "you taught me my letters in the Milborne Port Sunday-school. I am now a Methodist preacher, and I owe my success to you."

The incident affected me with gratitude. I was thankful that my short stay in the ministry had borne some fruit.

The thought of the expenses attending matrimony made me economical, and for the second time I walked to London. It was poor economy, for in so doing, I wore out a pair of shoes. I was now out of work, and upon reaching the city I bought out a coffee-shop, which I kept by myself until Christmas day, 1846, when I was married to Charlotte.

We had little time for honeymoon pleasures. We could not afford even a short wedding trip. I could not leave my shop, when rents, hired help and gas would consume all of my profits during my absence. My wife, Charlotte, came to my aid at once. We took hold of the matrimonial rope, and for forty-seven years, until death snapped the cord and separated us, we pulled together.

After two months' experience and some loss of money, we sold out the business, resolved to complete my long-cherished design of going to America — "the land of the free and the home of the brave." My brother Philip and my sisters Priscilla and Athaliah, then Mrs. Thomas Hinds and Mrs. Charles Garrett, were still living in London. We spent a short time visiting them before leaving England, and then prepared to cross the Atlantic.

A sailing vessel named the Royal Albert was about to leave for Quebec, and in April, 1847, we decided to sail by it to Quebec, Canada, and go from there to the United States. We hastily made the necessary arrangements concerning our baggage, and set sail from London the first day of May, 1847.

Two months were consumed in our passage from the London docks to Quebec. It was the period of the terrible ship fever, when many vessels lost their passengers; but, although there was much sickness aboard, we had no deaths on our ship. A babe was born to a German lady during the voyage, and we were all proud of the little extra passenger. I only suffered three days of sea-sickness, and gained in weight ten pounds during the voyage, but my poor wife nearly died of nausea.

On the banks of Newfoundland we were fog-bound, and drifted for an entire week. During the fog, a passing schooner ran into us and tore away our jib-boom, doing considerable damage, besides shaking up and frightening all of the passengers. I happened to be the first to see the passing vessel: its coming looked to me like a broadside. I hastily gave the captain the alarm, and he ordered the life-boats down, but we fortunately escaped shipwreck. After much noise, blowing of horns, and playing of bands by the Germans on board, the dense fog at last broke, and to our horror we saw that we had drifted near the bleak shores of Labrador. The captain turned deadly pale at our recent danger, and ordered the ship about. Although it was the month of June, ice and white frost were in sight. By skillful management we got out to sea again, where we were safe from grounding upon reefs. But a month had passed away; we had gone out of our course, and were still far from our destination. Now the two hundred Germans on board were out of provisions, and all of the passengers fell short of water. There was danger of serious distress.

The captain ordered the steward to allow the Germans only one sea biscuit, and each passenger a quart of water daily. Shifted about by contrary winds, we were filled with great anxiety for fear of possible starvation on the high seas.

HEZEKIAH BRAKE.

(At the age of 33 years.)

CHAPTER II.

CANADIAN EXPERIENCES.

We entered Quebec on a Sunday, and found a jolly people; as we passed many houses we could hear the sound of music and dancing. Of French descent, Roman Catholics in religion, they had probably attended religious services, made confession, and now, at ease regarding eternity, were devoting themselves to the enjoyment of time.

There were many stands along the streets where fruit, candies, and sour milk were sold, but passing these, Mrs. Brake and I entered a restaurant and enjoyed some excellent tea and cake. The delightful feeling of treading the solid land after a long sea voyage, none can know except those who have passed through the experience. When we went to the landing-place to secure our baggage, the scenes in sight would have aroused sympathy in the hardest heart. The infected ships swung idly at their moorings, waiting to be cleansed and disinfected. Many of them had lost nearly all of their emigrant passengers by ship fever, and the survivors were scarcely alive. As we stood listening to the sufferers mourning for their dead friends, one shipmaster said to me, as tears fell fast on his sunburnt face, "I have lost every Irish passenger." Although many years have rolled away, I have never forgotten the dirt, misery and sorrow connected with the fever scenes of 1847.

After a short time spent in looking at the old city of

Quebec, where we were especially interested by the awful guns of the battery, we ascertained that a boat, " Ireland " by name, was about to start for Hamilton City, on Burlington Bay, Upper Canada. We at once boarded a barge and were taken on the river to the place where the " Ireland " was moored, and a few minutes later were on our way up the River St. Lawrence.

Americans are familiar with the picturesque scenery of this noble stream, with the rivers which empty their swirling waters into its current; the Falls of Montmorency, where, eight miles from Quebec, one of these streams terminates, and the water, fifty feet wide, falls two hundred and fifty feet in a beautiful cataract; and of the old-time perils of the Lachine rapids; but to us these sights were new, and the inevitable spice of danger increased our interest. We stopped long enough in Montreal to visit the great cathedral, then one of the largest of its kind, and to note the thousands of barrels of flour on the wharves ready for shipment to London. Then we again committed ourselves to the mercy of the " Ireland."

At the foot of the Lachine rapids we found a very dangerous passage-way, as the canal around them was not yet completed. After a short interval of waiting, twenty fine span of horses were brought on the tow-path. When their traces were connected with our boat, there began the tug of war. Men hallooed, cursed, and whipped the horses. The boat seemed to us doomed. Unable to proceed, it was lost if it fell back. Tar barrels, every conceivable form of fuel used to increase the power and aid the struggling horses, seemed of no avail. Every face on board grew pallid with fear. To add to our terror we saw a small boat, containing two men, shoot with the rapidity of the current through the awful waters; who they were or what their fate we never knew. But at last the united efforts of captain, crew and canal-men were successful, and the rapids were passed. The beautiful Thousand Isles were soon left behind, and we launched our vessel on Lake Ontario.

The remainder of the journey was soon made. We passed Kingston as we entered the lake, then Prescott, Brockvale, and Old York, now the city of Toronto. From there we steered for the place of our destination — Hamilton, Ontario. During the entire journey, the beautiful shores with their nestling cities, the sparkling waters, and the cheer of passing boats, kept us in a state of constant delight.

Although in its extreme youth, Hamilton in 1847 was making a vigorous growth. Its inhabitants were enterprising people who had come to the New World to secure homes, and were fast building up a flourishing city. The Canadian pioneers were of every nationality, but were chiefly English, Dutch, Scotch, and Welsh. Hamilton was the home of Sir Allan MacNab, chief of the MacNab clan. His home was a beautiful castle, built after the fashion of those in Scotland.

Thus I became one of the early settlers of Upper Canada, and was actively interested in the development of the country. My wife kept boarders, and I secured a position as canvasser for headstones with I. Gardiner, a manufacturer of marble works in High street, Hamilton. Mr. Gardiner was an Englishman, and a very good designer in marble. He gave me twenty per cent. on all sales, and in canvassing the country for a distance of fifteen miles in every direction from home, I found him plenty of work.

The people of this region were social, hospitable, entertaining, and extremely loyal to Queen Victoria. They would keep me and my horse any length of time free of charge because I was an Englishman. My last work for the marble company was to put up a large monument for Major Shower's wife, in the Dundas churchyard. About the time my work began to be remunerative, my employer, who had fallen into debt, to escape imprisonment ran off to Buffalo. My occupation was now gone, and I turned my attention to helping my wife in the boarding business.

In 1848, the cholera in a very serious form visited Hamilton. During the time of the scourge, I remember meeting on the street two acquaintances, named Hull and Plowright. The latter complained of symptoms of the plague, and requested some burnt brandy. We went into the nearest saloon and procured the brandy, and then went home. A few hours later Mr. Hull came to my house and stated that poor Plowright was dead. There was no use now to avoid exposure; trusting to Providence to protect us, we went to make Plowright, who was a bachelor, ready for burial. In the morning we buried him without ceremony, and by the time I reached home I too was sick with the dreaded disease. I managed, however, to go to a doctor's, get some medicine and take it before I went to bed. My cure was amusing. My wife had hired my horse to a man to use for me, and shortly after I was taken with the cholera the animal came home without my cart. I went out and caught him, and the fright caused by the appearance of the runaway horse cured me. Perhaps I was frightened into the cholera — I certainly was scared out of it.

The Irish potato failure in Ireland, causing the terrible

famine of 1847, landed many Irish people in Canada; during the time from 1847 to 1849, Dutch immigration being also rapid, about three hundred thousand settlers came into Canada. Many of these pushed westward into Upper Canada, and from there emigrated to the United States. There were about a thousand souls in Hamilton in 1848-9. Now it is a city of ten thousand people.

My brother in London forwarded me a letter written by my mother during the year 1848, in which, after expressing surprise at my going to Canada, she said:

"If he is going to get land there, it may be like that his father bought at Milborne Port, in Somersetshire. That forty acres on which he built a house and spent so much labor and money, Sir William Medlicott has got and planted trees on it, and his father's family none the better for it. I think he would better have stayed at home. I say, I wouldn't go thousands of miles on a wild-goose chase to America."

From this letter I gathered that my mother wished me to come home. I resolved to sell out, and as she desired, return to England by way of the United States, ascertaining if possible in Albany the whereabouts of my long-lost father. It had been to seek him that I had first decided to visit the United States, and since I was to abandon my project of securing a home in that country, I at least could not return without taking my mother some information of the husband lost to her since 1832. So we packed such goods as we wished to take with us, called an auctioneer and sold the rest, and left the city of Hamilton.

We traveled by boat from Burlington Bay to Rochester, New York, and from there we were to go to Albany by way of the Erie canal, in order to see as much of the country as possible. We had a rough time crossing Lake Ontario, and every person on the steamboat was sick. But after a whole night's travel, we reached the opposite shore in safety, and on a Tuesday morning in May, 1848, we landed on United States soil.

CHAPTER III.

EASTERN OBSERVATIONS.

I had often dreamed of this free country, of which Englishmen sometimes remarked ironically that it was a land where there was no imprisonment for debt, but where every rascal found a loophole of escape from honest payment; but my heart swelled at the thought of standing upon ground sacred to liberty. Forty-eight years have come and gone since that May morning, and in all that time, America, sacred, as Marryatt says, to the eternal principles of right, has been my constant home, but her skies have never looked fairer, her breezes seemed balmier, than on that glad day when she first became my " ain countree."

As we had a day to spend in Rochester, our first experience was in changing our Canadian coin, of which we had quite a little sum, into United States silver. In order to facilitate matters in carrying it, we divided the money into two parts; my wife made a short, stout sack to hold her share of the silver, and I put the rest in my pockets. As purposed, we went by a canal-boat, and our fare for that long distance was only five dollars. There was only one passenger, the captain's wife, besides ourselves, and the crew consisted of the captain and one boy. Once safely embarked upon our tow-path excursion to the city of Albany, we were anxious to see the sights along our route, particularly the working of the locks. The heavy masonry which enabled the gatekeepers to raise the water in the locks at pleasure, the weirs, the lifting of boats to the plane desired, were new and interesting to us. The tow-path along the edge of the canal, the inevitable mule with the rope attachment to our boat, and the boy accompaniment riding leisurely along as the boat was towed onward, grew very monotonous, as did our three-miles-an-hour progress, but we enjoyed it all hugely, glad of an opportunity to see the new country. As I look back and think of the boy and the mule, I am reminded that, in his early youth, President Garfield followed the canal towpath as a mule-driver, and may have presented a similar appearance to the boy who accompanied our excursion.

Our extremely comfortable voyage had the monotony broken one morning by my wife exclaiming that her sack of money was gone. She had put it under the cushion upon which she slept, not noticing that slats formed the flooring. Upon raising the cushion she saw only the water; as luck would have it, however, the sack, which was tied in the middle, had caught on one of the slats, and although submerged, the money was safe. Poor Mrs. Brake was so nervous over the matter that during our journey she hardly recovered from the shock.

Through the courtesy of the captain and his lady, we were always given time to view the places through which we passed. As the canal skirted the cities of Lyons, Syracuse, Utica, Herkimer, Schenectady, and Troy, before we reached Albany we saw many interesting glimpses of these towns. Of all our varied experiences since leaving England, this long journey on a canal-boat was the most enjoyable.

However, the disagreeable will interfere, and the close of our journey proved this fact to be true. Having arrived at the last lock but one from the freight basin, I thought I would leave my wife on board and go on shore for an hour or so to hunt up a Hamilton acquaintance, whom I knew to be living near. During my absence, a heavy rain and wind storm came up, and when I returned our captain had gone through the locks and was near the place of landing his freight. Happening to know his sou'western broad hat, I found him, and learned where to find my wife and baggage. We could go no further that dark night, and were compelled to remain on board our canal-boat.

My father had been absent sixteen years; the anxiety of my dear mother, and her confidence in my ability to find her lost husband, made me anxious to begin the search for him. Once safely landed in Albany, my wife and I realized that it might take some time to accomplish the task, and in order to be able financially to succeed, I got a situation as waiter and my wife as pastry cook at the American Hotel in Albany.

I now began making inquiries for my father. The last letter my mother had received was written from a boarding-house, 23 Steuben street. In this letter he had said irreverently that he was going to send for all of his family in about six months, and they would all drink a bottle of wine together and sing a song of Zion in a strange land. No one seemed to have known him. One gentleman had seen a man answering my father's description at church once, but never afterwards. I examined the city records, and sought in every way to find a clue to his whereabouts. At last I gained the required information, and transmitted it to my mother in England. He had been last seen alive one morning in Steuben street, and in the evening found dead with the cholera upon the wharf; with many others who died of the plague, he was buried in a common grave. Thus, without even receiving the melancholy satisfaction of standing by his burial-place, ended the arduous undertaking of finding my father. The uncertainty of human life had never seemed so real to me as when I learned the certainty of his fate.

At this time the grand River Hudson literally teemed with life. On its broad bosom, floating palaces, unparalleled for grandeur and magnificence, and loaded with passengers to and from the Empire City, daily floated. Cities and towns had sprung up and were flourishing on its banks. A trip down this noble stream was like a journey through Elysium. My errand in Albany completed, I resolved to embark upon the Hudson and visit the great city of New York. Our baggage arranged and passage paid, we embarked on the "Palace," a boat whose elegance reminded me forcibly of the spacious drawing-rooms of London.

Once in New York, our attention was engrossed with the all-important subject, "Should we go back to England, or remain in America?" To me, aside from my mother's wishes, it seemed folly to return to England without having gained either knowledge or experience of a land which thousands boasted to be the best country on earth for a poor man. At this time hundreds of thousands of Europeans were annually coming into this country, and I believed that among them all there was a place for us. Our consultation ended in a mutual decision to remain; for me to visit the South, learn the character of the people, and the prospects there of earning an honest living for our family. Securing a suitable residence for my wife during my absence, I procured a ticket for a boat passage to Philadelphia, and started by way of that city to Richmond. After a two-days visit to Penn's old town, where her old governmental buildings and splendid system of waterworks were duly admired, I left the Middle States for the South.

CHAPTER IV.

SOUTHERN GLIMPSES.

On the way to Richmond, I stopped in the old city of Baltimore. It proved a very delightful place to visit, and the Barnum Hotel a scene of homely good cheer. The attention of the waiters, the kindness of the guests and the courtesy of the host quite enamored me with the Southern people. I made up my mind to settle in the South. Before leaving the city I visited its noted places. Of most interest to me were the two monuments of the Battle of 1814, and Washington. The first is fifty-two feet high, of Egyptian architecture, and is surmounted by a female figure — the genius of the city. It was built in honor of the defenders of the city in 1814. The other monument stands on an eminence, is two hundred feet high, and surmounted by a statue of General Washington. The whole design is of pure white marble.

Richmond at this time was the home of many rich, retired planters, and was a quaint old city. I reached it in time for the celebration of General Zachary Taylor's birthday, a short time previous to his inauguration as President of the United States. The citizens of Richmond gave a grand dinner to General Taylor at the National Hotel. As I was stopping there, I was one of the invited guests, and it was my pleasure not only to shake hands with the hero but to dine with him. During the after-dinner speeches, I formed exalted opinions of the United States. The fact that the curse of slavery rested like a blight upon this fair country was forgotten both by myself and the speakers. I resolved to remain in America, and no more reside in my native land. When the toasts were made and eloquently answered — a little worse, I must confess, for the champagne which flowed freely during the entertainment — I retired, greatly pleased, not only with the Southern people in particular, but with the United States in general.

On my stroll through the city the next day, my attention was attracted to the immense warehouses, and from these to the unfortunate slaves whose labor filled these buildings with the great Virginian staple — tobacco. Out of curiosity, I entered one of the slave marts on the main street, where an auctioneer was selling some slaves. A black woman was being sold away from her despairing husband and sobbing children; another slave — a tall, stout negro — was undergoing examination at the hands of the slave-buyer. The latter seemed in doubt about his soundness. As he punched the fellow in the stomach, and held his mouth open to examine his teeth, I ventured to ask what was his object in so doing. He replied:

"You ought to know that in a nigger every tooth is worth a hundred dollars."

The slave was bid off at two thousand dollars — a good price, I thought, for a man. I am sure if the author of "Uncle Tom's Cabin" had seen the separation of the helpless mother and children, she would have thought "truth stranger than fiction." Satisfied with this glimpse at the pet institution of the South, I returned to Baltimore. I took a great fancy to the town, and again stayed at Barnum's several days. While there, I met a planter who had just sold out his stock of slaves, and was looking for something in which to invest his money. He and I together leased the European Hotel, and went into business. On my way to Baltimore from Richmond, I stopped in the capital of the United States. During my three-days stay in Washington, I visited the capitol building. Nothing in its halls interested me so much as the portraits of Washington and Lafayette, in whose heroic characters I had always been greatly interested. At the White House I was shown all of the rooms and offices, and the contrast between English and American customs struck me very forcibly. I had once sought to view the interior of Buckingham Palace, but had been coldly refused admittance. It is needless to say that this courtesy increased my admiration for my adopted country. I ran down also to Mount Vernon, and visited the old farm-house and Washington's grave. In the house, in a glass frame, I saw the famous key to the Bastile. Washington's monument was then in course of construction. President Polk laid the cornerstone in 1848, but it was not finished for years.

As soon as we had completed our plans by paying an advance of fifty dollars, and agreeing to pay forty dollars per month for the hotel, we purchased the necessary improvements in the way of furniture, etc., and I sent to New York for my wife. At the same time I procured two bales of New Orleans moss, which made twenty mattresses, and these were placed in the bedrooms. We hired a black cook and a couple of mulatto maids to assist with the work, and in accordance with Southern custom we furnished, in addition to the ordinary accommodations, the doubtful one of a bar for liquors. As we had plenty of spare rooms for traveling-men, to show samples of their wares, and in every particular kept a first-class house, we soon had all of the patronage we wished. My partner, however, proved to be our best customer in the bar-room; so, leaving other business to him, I released him from that work, and for the first time in my life kept bar. The science of Temperance had made little progress with the general public in the year 1849. A hotel without a bar was not a matter of consideration.

As to servants, we hired slaves from masters, who collected their pay as they would for horse-hire. Female labor was very cheap, ranging from four to eight dollars per month. The morals of these slaves were of a low order, and they had to be closely watched to prevent them from stealing and selling knives, forks, plates, and other household articles. One night my wife took me into the cook's bedroom to see her. The woman lay on the floor in a state of maudlin drunkenness, and rats scudded away from her as we entered. By her side was an old teapot nearly full of ale, which she had stolen and carried up from the cellar in an old teakettle, and which she stoutly swore, when questioned, was nothing but water. Such was the character of much of the slave labor of that time. I little dreamed then that I should live to see the time when these neglected and often maltreated slaves would be emancipated, and liquor-selling, at least in my own State, prohibited.

It was not long before the evils of drunkenness presented themselves so forcibly to me that, despite the fact that in England I had always been accustomed to bars in public houses, I began to regret my entrance into hotel-keeping. Business always ran far into the night; my partner continued to drink heavily, and opposition companies of drunken firemen made the night hideous with false alarms and fighting. After four months of this vexatious experience, I settled my affairs, and moved with my wife (for we had no children) to Bergen, New Jersey.

CHAPTER V.

NORTHERN OCCURRENCES.

My experience in the South had satisfied me that we could not be happy there, and I decided to look for something to do thereafter in the North. I soon met an Englishman, who told me there was money to be made in the wool business. Accordingly I bought a horse and sent my new acquaintance to buy all the freshly-skinned sheepskins he could secure.

The method of treatment for the skins was as follows: As soon as they were brought in, the first one was laid with the wool downward and every part spread out. A mixture of lime, thick as whitewash, was then carefully spread on every part of it; a second and other successive skins were added, until a huge pile of them was heaped up. They were then removed, and the wool scraped off with a blunt-edged instrument like a drawing-knife. When the wool was washed, dried, and assorted, both wool and hides were ready for the New York market, where they always brought remunerative prices.

This business was carried on into the year 1850, when I discovered that my partner was not trustworthy. An examination into his sales showed that he had reserved from me ten dollars each week from his report, and this money I found had been forwarded to his family in England. So I quit the business, the unhealthy and offensive nature of which had thrown me into a malarial fever.

For two months I lived on my means; then Providence

again hunted me up. By searching the "want" columns of the New York papers I saw an advertisement for a man and his wife, the former to attend upon a rich, paralytical gentleman, and the latter to act as his housekeeper. We found the agent for the gentleman at the College Hotel, and he sent us to his employer's residence in Fifth avenue. We furnished the invalid with a recommendation from his physician, Dr. Valentine Mott, who had heard of us through Dr. Scott, of London, and also the following quaint testimonial as to our worth:

"Hezekiah and Charlotte
 Brake are Both
Worthy of Confidence.
           Sir John H. Beckles."

These proved satisfactory, and we were employed. We now settled our bills, and left Bergen, then a Dutch settlement containing a few small houses, and crossed by ferry from Jersey City to New York.

In our new home we found everything on a grand scale. In the richly-appointed house there were four servants under my wife's orders, while I served as nurse and attendant upon the sick man. The latter had two sons, seldom at home, and there was a lady connected with the family who owned two hundred and fifty slaves in South Carolina, and who spent the greater part of her time upon her plantation. Our situation had many difficulties, responsibilities and duties; especially was my own work tedious. I had unceasingly to rub the limbs of my helpless charge with a particular kind of ointment, and to give him only certain kinds of food and drinks. But my wife as housekeeper was in her element. We received good salaries, and were well contented.

By the end of two years, Mr. B., who was very patient, had recovered his health, and having by economy and self-denial, accumulated some money, I invested part of it in land at Hicksville and lots at Yonkers, on Oyster Bay, near Flushing.

My health now began to suffer from the close confinement I was undergoing. I had no opportunity to study the political conditions of my adopted country, and I began to meditate surrendering my situation and going into the country. The need of freedom from confinement and of country life for my health, made me long to secure land and go to farming. My wife, although reluctant to leave her comfortable situation, as usual acquiesced in my wishes, and it was so decided.

About this time there was a colony forming for the purpose of settling the Territory of Minnesota. I became interested in the meetings held for this purpose, and the speeches there made, so flattering to the new country, induced me to join the enterprise. A gentleman named George Bertram was made president and myself treasurer of the company; a committee was appointed and sent to Minnesota Territory to select a town-site and adjoining land for our farms. Thus, with about twenty other persons, I became a pioneer of a Northern State.

My mother in England, having heard of our wild project, sent me the following acrimonious epistle:

"March 1st, 1852; WALFORD GATE,
NEAR SHERBORNE, DORSET, ENGLAND.

"*Dear Son and Daughter:* I did receive your kind letter, after much anxiety. Was glad to find you and your wife in good health, and instead of going off into that terrible far-off Territory, not explored or inhabited, where nothing but trappers and Indians live, as I see by the map of the world. It will in the first place cost you, I fear, all your savings gathered together, money made at Baltimore and New Jersey, and what you have made in New York, and then be murdered in the wilds of Minnesota by savages, or drowned in Lake Minnetonka, or have your precious blood sucked out of you by mosquitoes — for a woman here told me they had trunks like elephants, and would do it. You must be crazy. You say you can get plenty of land there. Yes, no doubt you can; but you ought to recollect your father got 40 acres of land at Milborne Port. What good was it? You and he worked hard to make it of some use, and your father built a house on it, and now Sir William Medlicott has it all planted in fruit trees, and no one now belonging to him is any the better for it. My son, don't go there! If I can in England, with a family of nine children, save, and raise and support seven of them here, you can come back here and make your living. Your poor father left me in 1832; got to Albany; got overtaken with cholera, and died; and I now again thank you for the good you have done in finding out what had become of him in America. Of course, you are in pursuit of happiness — perfect happiness. But it is not to be found on earth.

"Write me again soon. My love to you both.

"Your affectionate mother, SARAH BRAKE."

My mother's letter greatly affected me, but it came too late to change my purpose. My plans were made; I had notified my employer of my determination, and notwithstanding his urgent entreaties for our continued service with him, and his generous offers to induce us to stay, I had agreed to start in a short time for our proposed town-site on the shore of Lake Minnetonka, in Minnesota Territory. When our luggage was packed and the dray came to remove it, my employer and I parted with mutual tears of regret.

We went by boat to Buffalo, where I hired a man and his wife to accompany us from there over Lake Erie, and around to Detroit; thence across Michigan by railroad to Chicago, Illinois. We stopped there for three days, and put up at the Lake Shore Hotel, then a very insignificant affair. We found Chicago a small town in a mud-hole. I was offered lots for two and three hundred dollars that since have sold for two or three hundred thousand dollars.

I went to Lake Michigan and found that my baggage, a burden of some fifteen hundred pounds, had reached there in safety. Where it was afterwards delayed I know not, but I had been in Minnesota three months before I received it. The cost of its transportation from New York to St. Paul was forty dollars.

A railroad had been started from Chicago to Galena, and was completed as far as Rockford, Illinois, a distance of some fifty miles. Rockford, although a town since 1832, was small, and gave no promise then of becoming later a prominent city through its watch industry. Upon arriving at this terminus of the railroad, we were seriously troubled as to how to proceed. At length, after much anxious perseverance, we succeeded in hiring wagons enough to carry Mr. Bertram, his wife and three children, myself and wife, hired man and wife, all of our luggage, and Mr. Bertram's dog.

To face the uninhabited waste before us required courage and determination, but, nothing daunted, early in the morning of May 10, 1852, we started, and moved forward until nightfall. The women would not go to bed: disgusted with the dirt and tobacco on the walls of our stopping-place, they sat up all night. But the men were tired; they ate their own cooking, admired each other, and retired to rest. They were pioneers. There was consolation in the thought.

There were no good roads then across these wilds, and there were many washed-out places in the way which caused us in passing over them to unload, walk across, and reload. After six weary days we reached Fever river, and there hired a barge to take us to Galena on the Mississippi.

The boat by which we expected to journey from Galena to Fort Snelling, Minnesota, delayed us two days by its non-appearance. This gave us an opportunity to see the sights of this city, built half upon and half under the overhanging bluffs of the "Father of Waters," as well as the lead mines of the vicinity. Few then had ever heard of the man who would render Galena historical from the fact that it was here he once lived; he who afterwards was the hero of Appomattox — General Grant. Even in 1860, "Captain" Grant was yet a teamster in Galena.

We employed part of our time in purchasing the necessary provisions to take with us to our far-away home. Two barrels of pork, one of corn meal, one of sugar, half a dozen hams and a chest of black tea were added to our stores. When the bill for fourteen persons (for to such dimensions had our party swelled), with extras for the ladies, was presented, it was truly alarming. My part of the sum was ten dollars, and I went deep into my pockets to find the necessary silver. The boatmen had stowed away the baggage by this time; we took our places on the boat and left the leaden country for golden prospects in Minnesota.

The boat by which we traveled was well equipped, furnished excellent fare and polite service. The journey of three hundred miles past the cities of Dubuque and La Crosse, the charming Lake Pepin, the fertile lands that spread out on either side of the noble stream, and the grand forests that constituted the hunting-grounds of Sioux and Chippewas, was truly enchanting, and formed a never-to-be-forgotten beautiful experience.

On June 24, 1852, our voyage ended, and we stepped ashore at Fort Snelling.

CHAPTER VI.

MINNESOTA PIONEERING.

In beginning this chapter, I am led to wonder what pioneers are to expect in return for the risks they run, the calamities they bear, the perils by land and water, the uncertainties of climate and soil, the loss not only of strength and treasure, but often of life itself. In reaching a new country, the seas of grass which stretch away into the infinite distance seem to rise behind one to the horizon and blot into oblivion, home, friends, vocation, while ahead they hide the future from the strained gaze. The rivers that must be forded, the dreaded savages which seem in imagination to be brandishing their scalping-knives on the opposite shores or on the rises of the prairie, make a climax of terrors, only surpassed by the horrors of life awaiting one from pests, famine, and often pestilence, in the new life beyond.

Fort Snelling, near the present important city of Minneapolis, was then the limit of northern civilization. Its commanding officer was Captain Steele. The site was on a fine plateau, stretching out to Crystal and Christmas lakes. Magnificent bridges now span the stream over which ferry-boats used to pass to St. Anthony's Falls, and the rapids are utilized for running mills which turn the wheat of the surrounding country into flour and the huge logs of the forests into lumber. The city of Minneapolis long since included St. Anthony within its limits, and only the Falls preserve the name of the old village.

In 1805, the United States purchased of the Sioux Indians a five-mile-square of land, including the beautiful Falls of St. Anthony, and in 1852 this was yet a military reservation. When we settled in Minnesota, Stillwater was the largest town and St. Paul was just coming into notice.

Many an hour when no noise or turmoil of traffic disturbed the sacred solitude, I sat on the bank of the river and gave myself up to the mystic influence of the Falls. I sometimes fancied that a phantom hovered over the waters, and the scene of a long-gone tragedy stood out vividly against the sky. The beautiful Dacotah maiden, whose lover-husband had deserted her for a new love, who sent her birch-bark canoe over the precipice and let the mad waters dash out her life, still seemed to haunt the place, and exercise a spell over falls, river, and shore.

But I have not mentioned how as a party we enjoyed the ride from Fort Snelling to St. Anthony. Constant exclamations at the beauty of the forest, the river, the lovely Falls of Minnehaha — the "Laughing Waters"— rang out. At last we stopped at the residence of Colonel Stevens, on the present site of Minneapolis. He entertained us until we could reach the place determined upon as our town-site, in the first house in Minneapolis. During our stay, he took us across the river to visit Governor Ramsay, the first Territorial executive of Minnesota, whose place was afterwards filled by Samuel Medary. The latter was one of the last Territorial Governors of Kansas. Governor Ramsay treated us very kindly. We dined with him in a little house not much like the usual gubernatorial mansion of to-day.

Leaving the women with our new friends, Mr. Bertram,

myself and two hired men sought a conveyance to take us to our proposed town-site. Colonel Stevens's brother owned a small saw-mill at the outlet of Lake Minnetonka, and kept there a small flatboat, which he loaned us. We loaded the boat with lumber and started up the lake to our new home, Excelsior, on Lake Minnetonka. Night overtook us, our boat leaked, and, despite our efforts at bailing out the water, we felt it about our knees, while the howling of wolves on the shores added to our terror and fear of landing. Our jolly boatman tried to cheer our fainting spirits by telling us there were no bears in the woods, and that the sounds we heard were made by big bullfrogs. He assured us further, that, far from being dangerous, their fat carcasses would sell for fifty cents apiece. Not particularly reassured, however, by his cheering words, we were glad when we reached our landing-place and had a rousing fire to frighten off the noisy beasts of the forest.

We took our lumber up a steep bank—afterwards called Brake's Landing—placed some boards slantwise upon tree branches, and with our faithful axes cut some wood for our fire, by which we heated our coffee and fried our bacon; after which, in our wet clothes, we lay down to rest. The excitement must have sustained us, for we did not catch cold. In the morning we made a shanty with bark sides, to be used for a temporary habitation, and cleared away the timber for a site for Mr. Bertram's home.

There were eight men by this time in our party. After a day's work and two nights of sleep, with the ground for a bed, three of our party went down on the boat for more lumber and other necessaries, and on reaching the saw-mill we took the opportunity to visit our wives at St. Anthony's. I found my wife in a comfortable home with the surveyor's wife, a Mrs. Christmas; but, to my surprise, Mrs. Brake was suffering with a severe illness, brought on by excitement. I made every arrangement I could for her comfort, and as soon as I could leave her I returned to the mill with the other men, bought the lumber, and took the "shakes" (clapboards) for Mr. Bertram's roof. As it was nearly dark, we remained with Mr. Stevens over night. After a good supper — for the new climate made us hungry as bears — we retired to rest. There were, twelve persons present, and the house only contained a small kitchen and a sleeping-room. Although everything was clean and neat, there was little space for hospitality. Necessity proved the mother of invention. The twelve persons were placed in two semi-circles on the floor, the women in one, the men in the other, the soles of the feet turned toward the center of the circle. In the morning, breakfast over, we bade our hospitable host good-bye, and headed our heavily-laden boat through the outlet into Lake Minnetonka.

So contrary was the wind, and so difficult the management of the boat, that, despite our efforts, we were driven to the wrong side of a strip of land which extended up the lake and was known as Meeker's Island, thus greatly increasing our distance.

On our way we passed Spirit Knob, a mound about twenty-five feet high, where the heavy timber began, and where deer and other game congregated. The Indians held Spirit Knob in reverence. For centuries they had buried their chiefs upon it, and the spirits of the dead were worshiped as protectors.

An old Indian fort on Meeker's Island also attracted our attention. It was built of slender logs set in a semicircle, as a screen against arrows, and had formerly been used by the Sioux as a protection against the Chippewas.

The boys, having believed us drowned, were more than glad to see us. They prepared a good supper, and around the evening camp-fire we recounted the adventures of the day. In about a week, President Bertram's two-roomed house was finished and occupied. As treasurer of the colony, it was conceded that the next house should be mine. Unfortunately, my wife's illness required my presence at St. Anthony. Dr. Ames, her physician, gave me no hope for her life, but by good nursing she recovered, and in two months could be removed to Excelsior. Other difficulties also confronted me. Birmingham, my hired man, who was heavily in debt to me, cut his foot while chopping, and immediately left for St. Anthony. But I plied my axe vigorously, and with the help of a man named Dan Farnham, soon had my house ready for occupation. Without my wife, the one-roomed log cabin with its outside kitchen canopied by the heavens was too lonely for me, and when we had made two bark shanties, one for Farnham and the other for a man named Roberts — whom we called "Robinson Crusoe" — we started out to explore the surrounding region.

We were greatly pleased with our new home. There were no enormous rents as in the East, and we had laid in a stock of provisions that lasted for some time. The lake abounded in fish, and in the forest any amount of game could be had for the shooting. Hunger is always good sauce, but our appetites here were truly voracious. "Robinson Crusoe's" shanty was on the margin of the lake.

Dressing himself in a buffalo-robe, he used to lie in ambush and shoot ducks enough to supply the whole party. A gun was a novelty to me, but I soon learned to shoot, and enjoyed the sport as much as the other boys. Squirrels and partridges were especially abundant, and we fairly reveled in our exchange of artificial city residence for genuine rural life. For some time we saw neither Indians nor the tracks of white men, and the magnificent timber of the well-watered fertile region impressed us much with the grandeur of the splendid yet lonely forest country about us. Returning from one of these excursions late one night, a terrible storm gathered over our bark habitations. The roar of the white-capped waves, the appalling thunder, the fearful blackness, relieved only by the vivid lightning, (for we could have no fire for the rain,) and the merciless torrents of water that poured in upon us through the curled-up bark of sides and roof, made us for the first time long for the snowy sheets and downy pillows of civilization. We had no change of clothing, and morning dawned before the storm abated so that we could make a fire and dry our clothing. We suffered no inconvenience, however, from the wetting, and, as soon as we were dry and had breakfasted, set about clearing up a spot for a garden.

In our wanderings, Farnham and I found a small canoe, which served us in many of our trips down the lake. All of my effects, including the goods purchased at Galena, were at Colonel Stevens's, and Farnham and myself early made a trip to the mill for supplies. We were not used to paddling a canoe, and came near getting upset several times before we reached the outlet of the lake. Arriving there in safety, we walked twelve miles to the Falls, where I found my wife convalescent. After two days spent in getting a team strong enough to haul my goods, we started home, which we reached before dark.

Crusoe's bark shanty was full of ducks he had killed during our absence, and the wolves had frightened him badly in their attempts to share them with him. Robinson had no notion of going through any more pioneer experiences, however, and, at his request, I took him with trunk and gun in my canoe to the mill, and from there he went to St. Paul, where he found work as a painter and remained as a resident.

Excelsior now began to improve. Mr. Bertram secured two yokes of oxen, and we were all benefited by the work of these strong, faithful animals. Strangers began to be attracted to our new town. Charles Galpin, of New York, a Baptist, was the first preacher in the new settlement, and we found him a great addition. His brother, George Galpin, a Methodist minister, followed him, and when a carpenter named McGrath joined us we at once decided that none of the elements was lacking for the building of a church. With the oxen we soon prepared a place for it. The building was a small frame one, concreted on the inside to shut out the cold.

By the time my wife could travel, we had cleared a patch of land, and had proudly sowed it in turnips. The meridian lines were run soon after, and I found myself in possession of a quarter-section of land fronting Lake Minnetonka. Our worst inconvenience now was from wet weather. Whenever it rained, we slept with an umbrella over our heads to keep the water out of our faces, or every shower would have given us a baptism. By dint of incessant labor we at last stopped the leaks, greatly to our comfort while in the house.

About the middle of September, a man named Buchanan visited Excelsior, and engaged in some speculations. Mr. Buchanan had married a New York actress, and wished to bring her to Minnesota. As there were no vacant houses in the village, I rented him a room in my new log house on my land. As I had sold my house in Excelsior to another new-comer, we moved into the farm-house before either of its four rooms was finished, and it took some time to "chink" the crevices with mud and cover the roof with "shakes." But when it was finished we had no repetitions of the umbrella experience. My goods reached us about the time we moved into the house. They had to be carted from St. Paul to Stevens's mill, and then brought by boat.

Mr. Buchanan and his newly-wedded wife arrived, and were greatly surprised to find a commodious, well-furnished room, with a good fireplace, in which to spend their honeymoon. Mrs. Buchanan had learned to smoke during her stage career, and at her request we smoked a pipe of peace on native Indian soil. This was the first romance in our colony, and all of us enjoyed it more than lovers of fiction enjoy the pages of a new novel. But the bride soon tired of the rustic surroundings, and persuaded her admiring husband to move to St. Paul, where her beauty and talents soon made her a fashionable favorite.

Our subsistence was now the question. We could not live like the Indians, on game and fish, and the novelty of woodland life was wearing off. We would need something more substantial than the autumnal beauty of the forest or moonlight upon the lake. So I set Charlie Herman, a great, strapping fellow, to work to clear up two acres of ground. But the possibility of a future crop could not provide for the emergencies of the present. Farnham, who had been a pioneer in the State of Maine, and whose claim lay by the side of mine, pointed out to me the fine sugar-maples among the timber. I was as simple as a child.

"Can we get some sugar out of *them?*" I asked.

Farnham laughed, and replied:

"You luny! didn't you know that? Why, we can easily make ten barrels of syrup out of those trees this winter, and sugar enough for years to come."

"But what can I do?" I asked. "I have no money to spare for help in doing the work, neither have I had any experience of it."

"Nonsense," he answered; "you have befriended me, and I am not going to desert you. If you want to go into this thing, I will help you, and we will make some money out of it."

"It will take money," I said; "but if you will help me, I will foot the bills. What shall we do first?"

"Build two sugar-houses," he replied — "one for boiling sugar-water, and one for finishing off. We can make 'shakes' for a covering for them. We will want Russian iron enough to make two boilers, and something to hold the sugar-water after it runs from the trees."

A happy thought struck me.

"I'll get some canoes," I said, (the Indians had left a lot of them on the shore of the lake,) "to hold the water, and I will go to St. Paul and buy some barrels to put the rest in; but what will we put under the trees?"

"Troughs, of course," laughed Farnham; "we can hew them out of linn or basswood, five hundred of them; and we will make a thousand spigots, too. There is plenty of sumach around here for *them*. It will give us plenty of amusement for the fall and winter."

And so it was settled, and our work for several months ahead was now planned.

While we were doing our first year's work, we did not have to do without fruit, for above us was a small lake, a mile long and half a mile wide, which we called "Charlotte," after my wife, and on its margin was a cranberry marsh which provided us in the berry season with an abundance of fresh, ripe fruit.

We heaped up the logs and brush from our clearing. While these heaps burned, we got out the blocks for the shingles to cover our sugar-houses, and made every preparation possible for sugar-making.

During all this time, although many persons had arrived in and settled around Excelsior, and the business of clearing up farms was going rapidly forward, we suffered many deprivations. One of these was for milk and butter, as there was not a cow within twenty miles. As I had no horse, I went on foot in search of a cow. I found one for sale near St. Paul, and paid sixty dollars for her. I had thirty miles to drive her, and it took me three days from the time I left to get home. Half way, I thought I would rest myself and the cow. Throwing myself down under a tree, I fell asleep, and the wicked creature took advantage of my slumber to depart without bidding me good-bye. When I woke up there was nothing to be done but to go back to St. Paul, pay for a night's lodging for myself and for the cow's extra keep, and take a fresh start in the morning. The cow did not get out of my sight the rest of the way, and at midnight I reached home and put the animal in the new stable Farnham had built during my absence. Our new acquisition proved a valuable one, and we were now much more comfortable.

Winter fell upon us early in November, but our ready axes and adzes already had hewn out our troughs, and cut the lengths of sumach for spigots. With our prospective comfort from good food and warm fires before us, we were quite ready to go under shelter. During the cold weather, we worked in the house at the spigots. They were seven inches long, and three inches were left round for insertion into the tree. The pith was bored out of the end to be inserted, and the rest of the spigot was sloped off, and a groove made for the passage of the sugar-water from the tree to the trough.

The winter was very cold, the thermometer sometimes registering forty degrees below zero. We had raised little during the year, and there was much suffering for the necessaries of life in the new colony. I cut slough-grass for my cattle, and they lived through the winter and fared very well. My wife suffered much from the severity of the climate, and we were all glad when February came.

While we were busy with the sugar work, a company of twenty Sioux Indians visited our camp, and overran my house. My wife showed no fear of them, and they quite amused me, but several of our people hid until the Indians were gone. Our furniture, particularly the carpets and rugs, delighted the wild creatures, who had come from a camp, named for their chief—"Shockapi." When they saw themselves reflected in a large pier-glass, they nearly went into fits of ecstacy. The braves were painted black, white, yellow and red, and the squaws, save for a sort of apron, were entirely nude. They were beauties long remembered. They bought fifty cents worth of pork of me, and going out to some logs, they piled up chips and cooked a sort of pudding they called "tooley." They were as happy as clams while they ate it, and then the big braves rested while the squaws cut down a great tree I gave them. In the morning, these worthies went down the lake, and the poor squaws hewed out a canoe, made some paddles, and that night by the light of the moon rowed after their lords and masters. We saw them no more. The military authorities at Fort Snelling sent out troops in various directions to watch the Indians, and this perhaps had much to do with their peaceable visits to white men.

Once after this — in the following summer — Shockapi and fifty or sixty of his tribe came to my cabin. We were eating dinner, and we went on with our meal, paying no attention to the wild words and gestures of the chief and his squaw. Meanwhile, the other squaws put up tents all around us, and Lottie was frightened when the old one mentioned walked in, picked up our teapot and motioned for some tea to be put into it. Then, seizing a knife, fork, plate, cup and saucer, she marched off with the spoils to her tepee, where a little later we found her dining in great style. The rest of them were engaged in pulling up all my squash- and pumpkin-vines, and in cooking the fruit in their dirty kettles.

I had earnestly entreated Captain Steele of the Fort to have the Indians removed from the neighborhood, and hearing of the order for their removal, Shockapi had come to sell me his canoes and to show his resentment. He now called them all before him and made a long oration. Tears rolled down their swarthy cheeks as his eloquence grew more powerful. I knew enough of their language to know that he was telling them that they were leaving forever their favorite hunting-grounds, where they had so long enjoyed freedom and happiness. I bought all of their paddles and canoes, and the Indians departed. Poor Shockapi! I pitied him and his friends from my heart.

By the first of March we needed vast hogsheads for the supply, and had only a few barrels. Farnham and I started in different directions to look for something that could be converted into use, and were fortunate enough to find several large Indian canoes. We took them into the camp just in time to save the sugar-water. We had spent a week boring the trees, inserting spigots, placing troughs under the five hundred trees, and stopping leaky spots in the canoes. The snow was cleared away, and we worked briskly amidst the crackling and popping of thawing trees and the constant crashing and thundering of the breaking ice on Lake Minnetonka. By the first of April, we had begun the sugar-making in earnest, and the work of collecting the syrup, boiling it down, straining and skimming it, occupied all of our time, except snatched moments when we shot squirrels for a change, these little creatures being very plentiful.

I used to wonder, as we worked in our lively camp, if Father Hennepin, in his exploration of other and perhaps better worlds, looked down sometimes upon the county in Minnesota which bore his name, and saw his successors early trying to draw sweetness from the somber forest through which as an earthly pilgrim he had strayed. For our camp had become quite famous, and merry parties of pleasure-seekers came from St. Anthony and St. Paul to visit us. Work by night as well as by day was necessary, and the great fires, the interested faces about them, the black shadows of the forest, doubly intensified by the flame and smoke, and the sounds of the night heightened by the roar of the grinding ice, formed a never-to-be-forgotten experience. Many of the visitors to our camp brought with them not only luncheon, but brandy. They mixed it with maple syrup, and under its exhilarating influence they told stories, sang gleeful songs, and in the morning went off declaring themselves delighted with camp experience. Some insisted that we were doing wonders in these woods; others envied our success, and predicted speedy failure. But as early as the 25th of March, 1853, we had produced a barrel of genuine maple syrup, for which a St. Anthony merchant, who was in our camp, not only paid us a dollar and a quarter a gallon, but engaged all we could make that spring. He sent us four empty barrels, and by April 10th we had filled them, and received two hundred dollars for their contents. Up to the last of April our work continued, gradually decreasing, until at last the sap got up in the trees, the sugar-water stopped running, and we put away our spigots, troughs, and canoes, and plugged the holes in the trees. Our sugar work was over for that year. Of the energy, perseverance and labor required to make a success of it, no idea can be given.

The merry month of May was ushered in in Hennepin county to the sound of the chopper's axe, of falling trees, the plowman's cry to his oxen, and the merry voices of a happy people, who realized that their home was a paradise on earth, and if its soil could only be brought into the proper conditions, would prove a veritable Eden in its productiveness. Several small houses had been built in Excelsior, the lots cleared of timber and converted into gardens, where women planted garden seeds and flowers, and all anxiously prepared for the expected harvest. Municipal matters were discussed as assiduously between the pauses of axe and adz as in New York or Boston. Mr. Galpin preached to us every Sunday, and reminded us that we were Christians though we lived in a wilderness, and that we must make the town what its name implied. Many children were now in the neighborhood, and a school-house was built and a teacher employed to teach them.

While the ground was too cold for corn, we planted potatoes, turnips, and other vegetables, and I made a hot-bed, and early had cabbage plants ready for transplanting. I made a fence of pickets around my garden, and was rewarded for my labor by raising from the Jenny Lind variety of potatoes six hundred bushels to the acre. The changes from cold to heat and from heat to cold were remarkable for their rapidity. So oppressive was the heat during part of the time that the oxen often laid down, completely overcome. We planted our corn with the hoe.

Our small clearing planted, Farnham and I built us a boat and explored the lake-shores. Meeker's Island (afterwards bought by Farnham) was also visited. We were horrified to witness, during one of these excursions, a brutal murder. A party of Sioux Indians, then on the war-path against the Chippewas, had captured one of the latter tribe and fastened him to a tree on the island. Around him they had piled brush and other dry materials which they had ignited, and the flames were leaping up around the doomed Indian. Powerless to avert the holocaust, we watched the terrible scene with a fascination impossible to describe. The leaping, shouting savages in their hideous war-paint and feathers, the stolidity of the victim, thrown into relief against the gloomy background of sky and forest by the flames of the funeral pile, held our attention until it was almost too late to push away unseen in our canoe. In the morning, we visited the spot where the crime occurred, removed the still smoking fagots and found bits of human bones, a finger-joint, and part of a skull. But for this, we might have believed the scene of the previous night but a dream. Sick with horror, we were glad to leave the place and go on to the Minnetonka mill-house.

The lake was still full of blocks of floating ice, and our boat was too frail to carry a burden in its waters; so we borrowed Mr. Stevens's boat again, and took with us a load of lumber. We progressed rapidly until we left the outlet of the lake, a distance of two miles, passed Spirit Knob in safety, and would soon have reached Brake's Landing, had not contrary winds driven us back. Although late in the spring, the ice ground against our boat in masses, threatening to overwhelm us in the water. Neither of us had much knowledge of managing a boat, and the consequence was we were driven to shore opposite Meeker's Island, seven or eight miles from home.

The prospect of spending the night in this wild region, surrounded by panthers, wolves, and other dangerous animals, (to say nothing of Indians,) in our wet clothing, and without food, was far from pleasant. To encounter the raging winds and the thick darkness of the lake, was not to be considered. Better a death upon *terra firma* at the hands of Sioux or Chippewas, than a watery grave in Minnetonka. We had no guns with us, but we fortunately had a knife, axe, and a few matches. We fastened our boat, gathered some dry wood in the darkness, and made a fire, by which we spent the night. Sleep was out of the question. There were noises of all sorts about us. Besides the roaring waters, wolves howled, and the woods seemed full of sounds; and, as I sat smoking by the blazing fire, brooding over our danger, and my wife's fears for my safety, I wished most heartily that I had never undertaken the life of a pioneer.

After daylight, we found an abandoned shelter near by, where some enterprising person had evidently tried to prove up on a claim, and left it in disgust. A few kettles and a couple of buffalo-robes were all that remained of his deserted furniture. We wrapped ourselves up in the robes and dried some of our garments by the fire before we started home.

During the night I had asked Farnham to sing us a song, to pass away the time.

"Song be d—d!" said Farnham; "we have too many songs about us now. Wouldn't we look great, singing songs of Zion beside these strange waters? No siree! I've hung my harp on the willow!"

In the morning, when our boat was headed homeward, and the wind had fallen — making our passage comparatively safe — Farnham, hoping to have some fun, said to me:

"Sing us a song, Brake; we seem now to be all right."

"Not much," I answered; "I am too hungry for music."

"But it will pass off the time," he said; you know, I have heard you say that you sang 'Row, brothers, row,' on your way up the St. Lawrence, some years ago. I know you can sing."

"I did," I replied, "but I was younger then, and had not fasted twenty-four hours in wet clothing, without shelter; besides, I haven't forgotten Jerusalem, and I will not sing by the waters of Babylon."

We were almost starved, and woefully jaded, when at last we reached the presence of my distracted wife. As soon as I could assure her of our perfect safety, we ate ourselves nearly to death, and then went to sleep. Our slumbers were so protracted that my wife became alarmed for fear we would never wake again; but, as usual, our exposure and danger left us unharmed.

We had bought the lumber to make us a boat, and as soon as our sturdy hoes had headed off the weeds in garden and field, and the seeds for summer plants, such as squashes and other vines, had been sown, we finished our craft. We made a box to trail behind, put our fishing-tackle in the boat, and tried our luck at fishing. The evening usually proved the best time for the sport. In two hours we could catch enough fish to last us a week. They were mostly bass and pickerel, very fine and fat. We always threw them into the box of water, where they would live for a week at a time. We sometimes saw Indians on the lake, and they often persisted in fastening our boat to theirs and towing us down stream, greatly to my wife's terror.

By July, there were some seventy-five persons living in our neighborhood. Some of these early pioneers deserve especial mention. A gentleman from Clinton, Illinois, named Peter Gideon, laid out the first orchard, became well known as a fruit-raiser, propagated the "Wealthy" apple, received encouragement in his work from the State, and made Hennepin county his permanent home. A Mr. Hull, a Universalist preacher, who settled there at the same time, started the first ferry. It was on his claim at the Narrows, a strait between the upper and lower divisions of Minnetonka.

The experiences of the previous year repeated themselves. In addition to our other work, Farnham and I built a house and dug a well for a man named Latterner. We also cleared ten acres of land for him. This new land produced eighty bushels of corn to the acre the following year, and the grain sold for a dollar a bushel.

Grasshoppers visited us in the early fall of 1854, and destroyed the corn crop.

Winter set in early in November, and by December the snow was four feet deep. A terrible blizzard, lasting forty-eight hours, struck our county in January, 1855. With the snow so deep it was almost impossible to care for our stock, the thermometer forty degrees below zero, the bitter storm still raging, while even by a red-hot stove people were chilled with the cold, it seemed our most cruel experience. When the storm abated, the oxen and cow were safe, but nearly all our chickens were frozen to death.

Minks and rats were so plentiful that the few remaining chickens soon met a bloody fate from these animals. Cats there were none. Parties living in Excelsior offered a dollar apiece for these domestic creatures, and upon the advent of the first one it was hailed as a deliverer.

The clearing of the blocked-up roads took some time. My oxen proved of great value in this work, and I freely devoted them to the public service.

About this time the first store was started in Excelsior, and we were enabled to buy our groceries without going all the way to St. Anthony or St. Paul—Minneapolis not then being in existence, except for a few frame houses near the west side of the river opposite St. Anthony. A little later, however, a fine bridge spanned the river.

Our first lawsuit was over the oxen, whose services we had all found so indispensable. They had been purchased by Mr. Charles Galpin, and I bought them of him. An officer of the law who had been instructed to collect some indebtedness of Mr. Galpin in New York, served a garnishment against the payment of the money, and, greatly to my annoyance, an action was immediately brought in court. Mr. Galpin won the case, and I paid him, keeping the cattle. The suit caused the first ill-feeling in the settlement.

The spring of 1855 found us all busy extending our clearings, and Farnham and myself, who were still partners, under contract to build some good log houses for a party of New England people. I had found and hired a stout Irish boy named Pat Murphy to stay with my wife and assist her with the gardening.

On the first day of May I took the oxen and traveled northward into the big woods. There were no roads, but we had previously blazed the trees to the locations, and, as I carried a pocket compass, we were not afraid of getting lost. No surveys had been made here except the running of the meridian lines. The timber was so thick that it took some time to clear a place for a house. A week of arduous labor in the dense, lonely forest made us rejoice when the Sabbath dawned. We did not listen that day to Henry Ward Beecher or Dr. Tyng, neither did we sit during service in a grand cathedral amidst the arches of whose vaulted roof the grand tones of a mighty organ reverberated, and the sweet sounds of cultured voices lingered; but in our little plain chapel a plain man preached to us plain truths, and we all joined heartily in the simple hymns, and rejoiced in the thought of the poet, that 't was —

"Sweet on that sacred Sabbath Day,
That day of calm and holy rest,
From earth's wild cares to soar away,
To think of regions pure and blest;
Far off to wing our spirit's flight
To sparkling realms of purest light."

The two cabins, which were finished in a couple of months, would hardly please the eye of the fastidious resident of to-day. And yet they were strong, well built, and comfortable. They cost fifty dollars apiece; were made of hewn logs, covered with "shakes," and had each a boarded door six feet high and three feet wide. The apertures between the logs were "chinked" with stones and chips, and filled in with mud.

When the families had occupied these cabins, we built a third for one of their friends. As it was only about three miles from home, we walked there in the morning and returned late at night. We always carried our guns with us, as wolves frequently followed us. I owned about half a dozen good-sized pigs at that time, and they took to following us. The constant squealing and grunting they kept up in their attempts to keep us in sight, frightened away the wild animals both going in the morning and returning at night, for the pigs stayed in sight, eating mast, all day. Pat facetiously declared we were well protected by both a van and a rear guard, besides carrying English, American, and Irish "arms." My own arms often ached too wearily to care for Pat's commentaries. But it was true that wild-cats, wolves, and even owls, kept still while those shoats squealed. They were all doubtless paralyzed with shame that their whole chorus could not make as much noise as five pigs.

I now sold my cattle, and purchased a yoke of steers of Mr. Bertram. At a great sacrifice, I paid for them by deeding him seven lots on Oyster Bay, near Flushing, but I needed the oxen more than the lots. I decided to start a new settlement, perhaps near Buffalo Lake, and went down to St. Anthony and persuaded several men to join in the scheme by promising to conduct the business, as Mr. Farnham had gone upon his claim. A meeting was held at my house near Excelsior a week later, and the arrangements were made.

Mr. Langdon, one of our company, being ill, we postponed our plans for ten days, during which time I turned my attention to our crop. The time had been so fully employed that it was now the 20th of June, and too late for clearing land for corn-planting. But I saw that a patch of partly-cleared land could by some work be utilized for sowing corn broadcast for cattle-feed.

We yoked the cattle and went out to survey the field. Pat evidently did not relish the log-rolling and burning. He scratched his head and said comically —

"I've something in me head, Mr. Brake."

"So I would suppose," I answered.

"An' did ye niver hear of Mr. Fox and what he said to a lady? That's a sort of quotation."

"What was it Pat?" I asked.

"Why he wor' payin' his respects to the lady, an' she told him she did n't care for him the weight of a creeper. She wor' playin' with a creeper flower, an' meant *that*."

"And what did Mr. Fox reply, Pat?"

"Och! he just wrote in her album these very appropriate words, of which I've been makin' a sort of translation:

"'I forgive you, dear lady, for what you have said;
Women will talk of things that run in the head.'

"I've got somethin' now runnin' in me head, an' like a woman must talk of it. What do ye say to a loggin' bee?"

"I say it is a happy thought, Pat," I replied, "and we will have one."

So we had an old-fashioned log-rolling. Three of our neighbors came with their teams, and while the women visited, and prepared us excellent dinners and suppers, we had a merry time heaping up and burning the great fires. In two days the work was done, and Pat scratched his head with increased satisfaction. It seemed almost a sin to destroy the magnificent timber, but we could neither sell nor use it, and were obliged to burn it in order to plant the land. When the fires were out, I sowed the corn and Pat harrowed it in, and as a rain fell just after, in an incredibly short time our brush-patch was converted into a green and growing field.

Visitors now were plentiful in Excelsior; dozens of persons, attracted by the scenery, the hunting and fishing, camped on Lake Minnetonka, or floated about in boats on its waters. A boarding-house was opened, a saw-mill started, and a doctor settled among us. So healthy was the climate that Dr. Snell turned 'squire, and again so peaceable were the people that this profession paid no better than the first. The beautiful forests, the inspiring breezes, made our new settlement so near a Utopia that I sometimes questioned the statement made by my mother:

"You need not expect perfect happiness; it is not to be found on earth."

Dr. Snell's first patient was treated in my house. Mr. Lock, one of the gentlemen for whom the cabins were built, had an artist friend from Philadelphia visiting him. The artist, Joseph McLeod, was taken very sick, and Mr. Lock brought him to my home, where I nursed him back to health.

This incident proved of great benefit to me. The members of his family became our friends, and were ready in every way possible to show their gratitude. Joseph McLeod, afterwards known as Judge McLeod, was a devout Episcopalian, and when he learned that while in New York I had been a member of the Episcopal church, he sent his pastor — the Rev. Mr. Chamberlain — up to see me. We united our efforts, and built a log building for a church of our own denomination, and Mr. McLeod aided the work by beautifully painting the windows.

When the scheme for the new settlement had taken definite shape, I went, although without money, to St. Paul — where, through the courtesy of these friends, I had unlimited credit — to select axes, grubbing-hoes, cooking utensils, and a tent, for our camping expedition. On the way I stopped at Crystal Lake to water the oxen. While they were resting I discovered the nest of a huge snapping-turtle. Knowing that the thirty eggs in the sand would hatch by means of the heat of the July sun without the aid of the mother turtle, I thought I would take her to the hotel with me, where the dollar and a quarter received for her would settle my bill. As I threw her into the wagon she gave a snap, and I thought my thumb was gone. It proved to be my thumb-nail only, but before I got it wrapped up, my friends — the cattle — deserted me, as friends usually do when one is in trouble. I have never yet been able to decide which is the harder on piety —the vindictiveness of a snapping-turtle, or the perversity of a stubborn yoke of oxen. I found the animals peacefully slumbering in the lake, and had to wade into water up to my neck to goad them out. The mud of these banks was the blackest I have ever seen, and we presented a black and sorry spectacle when at last we started on our journey.

When we reached the foot-bridge half a mile from the Falls of St. Anthony, the cattle refused to go upon it. They rushed down a steep bank into the water, and before I could stop them had nearly entered the swift eddies of the rapids. Luckily, the water was only up to my armpits, and by stumbling over the rocks I at last goaded them up a steep bank, went a quarter of a mile around to get a road, and got back to the ferry. Five or six men came to my assistance, but again the cattle went through the same performance. I tried again, the third time, and in this trial got them on a barge and across the stream. I was sure now that cattle had the advantage of turtles in fitting a man for the world which the foaming, swirling waters illustrated. I looked with a softened feeling toward the turtle, the wicked cause of all my trouble. It was not there! It had taken advantage of my perplexities, and escaped along with my temper, near the Falls. I never saw it again. But night came on before I reached shelter, and I was obliged to lie down in my wet clothes, without bed or food, while the oxen rested or ruminated throughout the night in the surrounding forest.

In the morning I soon reached the home of Mr. Roberts, once our "Robinson Crusoe," where I ate a hearty meal, and then proceeded on to Mr. McLeod's store, made my purchases, and, after stopping in St. Anthony long enough to see the parties interested in the new settlement, returned home.

This new settlement was to be in Hennepin county, about eight miles from my home. Charlie Herman and I had blazed the trees to the location, and taken a survey of the surroundings. An immense thicket covered the spot, and a swamp had to be crossed to reach it. An overland route to it would have to be made before any effective results could be obtained. By crossing the lake at Mr. Hull's ferry, we reached a ridge of land along which we could easily travel by the lake for some distance without getting into the water. The view from here was most enchanting, and we hardly knew whether to be surprised or amused, when, upon reaching the point where we left the lake, we saw some writing pasted upon a tree, which read as follows:

"Turn, Turn, Accursed Stranger, Turn!"

We did not turn, but ate our luncheon, and traveled on, marking out our road, clearing brush, blazing trees, and making the best of the discomforts of such work, under a fierce July sun. We had to "corduroy" (that is, cut some small logs and lay them side by side and throw brush and dirt over them) a swamp, and then a mile further reached the edge of a thicket. As leader of the expedition I assigned each man a "length" or a certain part to clear, and we worked assiduously until night.

We built a great fire, ate our suppers, and slept soundly upon the ground. In the morning we resumed our work, and in about two hours finished cutting our way through the thicket, and reached a fine open prairie. As there was no water here, we only stayed long enough to eat our breakfast, and then made our way on two miles further. Here we reached a small lake, and the place selected for our destination. Surveys subsequently located this spot as section 13, township 100, range 24, in Hennepin county. All expressed themselves as satisfied with the location. It was a truly beautiful spot. The clear waters of the little lake abounded in fish; the timber was not too thick; the growth of fine walnut trees was interspersed with wild apple-trees laden with fruitage, and the region seemed well calculated to afford a fine pastoral country. All agreed to have the location surveyed, to take claims, build houses, and make for themselves homes in what would then be the second interior settlement in Hennepin county, Minnesota.

In about a week, I secured the services of Surveyor Christmas, of St. Anthony, and six men to aid in the work of clearing the land for the new settlement. The men were to do the work and I was to board them. Pat Murphy was to take the oxen along to haul heavy timber out of the way. A day was agreed upon as the time of starting, and a place appointed for a rendezvous. Every man was present, and we began work. In three days the road had been surveyed and worked, and we could go with a team from Excelsior to the site of our new village. A little later, by the aid of my oxen in hauling the timber, four log cabins had been built.

So much care in providing provisions and other necessaries devolved upon me, that I was obliged to have one of the men do the cooking, and I spent most of my time in going back and forth. In order that the building might go rapidly forward, I let the men use my team and I tramped the distance with a sack upon my shoulders, containing the articles needed.

On one of these trips, having started late in the afternoon, it grew dark and I lost my way. The horrors of a night alone in a dense forest in an unsettled part of the country were before me. I could hear the wild-cat scream and the wolf howl, but for fear of the swamps which surrounded me I dared not go forward. I had an axe and matches with me, and built a fire. Through all that long night I gathered brush and heaped it upon my fire. I did not dare to sleep, so I sang loudly, "Row, brothers, row!" and wondered if the stream of life was not running fast to the ocean of death — but no one came to keep me company. Perhaps the music scared stray travelers away. I might, if seen, have been taken for a wild man of the forest.

At last the most welcome dawn I ever saw gilded the eastern sky, and, finding my bearings, I trudged joyfully homeward. When, late in the afternoon of that day, with about forty pounds of provisions in the sack on my back, I found my way into the camp, the hungry men made the woods ring with hurrahs.

Mr. Langdon attended to the building of his house, but two men named Foster wanted me to take my young oxen and go up to Forest Dale and assist in building their cabins. It was the middle of September, and I had been having a brief rest at my home near Excelsior. I was now a citizen of the United States, having taken out my papers, and was anxious to show my interest in the welfare of the country by participating a little in political affairs. My home, too, needed attention, and I was heartily tired of pioneering; so I hardly relished the new work.

Somewhat reluctantly, and with Pat's assistance, I yoked up the oxen, put a sack of provisions around the yoke, and started on foot for the new town-site. We went to the ferry, but Mr. Hull would not take us across the Narrows with the oxen. The water was about three rods wide and fifteen feet deep. We must get across somehow, or else go a long way around.

"Pat," I said, "you jump on one of them and ride over."

Pat looked at me dubiously, and then laughed.

"No sirree," he said; "I've me first time to be drowned, and I niver mane to have me last."

"But you won't drown," I said; "you ride to guide them, and I will follow in the boat and urge them over."

"Urge me over, you mane," said Pat. "The water's too cold for bathin', I'm thinkin'."

"But the water is warm, Pat," I urged; "it wouldn't hurt you to fall into it. We would pick you right up. You would not know how to drive them forward if they balked. Do get on one of them."

"By your l'ave, no," said Pat; "I'm no swimmer, and I'd rather not risk your pickin' me up. If I kape on the ferry-boat there'll be no need of troublin' ye to jump in after me. Besides, the near ox don't like me because I'm an Irishman and believe in shillalahs. He might just hold his head down, and then trample me under his feet. Thank ye, Mr. Brake; I'll be ridin' on the ferry, if ye've no objections."

Clearly, there was no use to argue with Pat. There was no alternative. I said to Mr. Hull, "You come alongside of the oxen with the boat; if they balk, take your stick and drive them over." I then jumped on the near ox and started. They went down into the water until only their noses were visible, and there was less than common to be seen of myself; but I rode over in safety, and the oxen seemed to enjoy the journey. When we landed on the other side, Pat looked at my dripping garments, and his laughter exploded. It did not make me any better humored.

"It wouldn't have hurt you to have ridden over," I said. "It was cowardly to refuse. A boy should never be afraid of a wetting."

"If ye plaze, Mr. Brake," said Pat, with a twinkle in his eye, "I *rowed* over, and I'd rather be a coward for the distance of three rods than a dead Irish lad all the rest of the journey of me life."

Pat's philosophy was unanswerable; and after borrowing a change of clothing of Mr. Hull, we started upon the margin of the upper lake. The oxen could not travel upon the ridge, and we were obliged to keep in the water at the edge of the lake. It was from two to three feet deep, and presented a waving appearance from the great waves surging against the shore. Pat and I had another altercation. Wouldn't he ride, as I had done at the Narrows?

"Thank ye, no," said Pat from the ridge; "I prefer walkin', and I'm very comfortable where I am."

"Well, hand me a stick," I said, "to keep them from getting out of their depth."

He did so, and we proceeded up the lake — he upon the dry ridge, and I astride the near ox.

About half-way up the margin, the cattle became uneasy. Across the lake, four miles off, could be seen a beautiful table-land covered with exquisite verdure. Whether or not the cattle decided that they would seek this oxenian paradise, or whether the distance lent an enchantment that bewitched them, I do not know; but one thing was certain, "forgetting the things behind them," in spite of winds or waves, they dashed forward toward the prize. Poor Pat stood on the ridge and yelled "Murder!" at the top of his voice, and consoled me with the confidential statement:

"You 're sure to be drowned, Mr. Brake. You 'll niver see the dry land any more. Och, murder! murder!"

A hundred rods from the shore, in water fifteen feet deep, their heads still turned to the pastures green, the cattle began to show signs of exhaustion. Pat, frightened at being left on the lonely shore alone, was screaming louder and louder, when, all at once, as if disgusted with his yells, the brutes wheeled around and made straight for the spot where he stood. Pat was so disconcerted at the effect of the sound of his voice that he called out, "Holy Mother!" and came near falling upon his head into the water before he could get out of the way. The rest of the distance was traversed without accident, and around the supper-table we all laughed at the adventures of the day. Pat's equanimity was perfectly restored. The boys rallied him on his heroism.

"I 've always remarked," answered Pat, "that when I 'm alive at bed-time, I 'm apt to be stirrin' in the mornin'. As I was tellin' Mr. Brake, it 's better to be a coward eating praties at supper than a hero with fifteen feet o' water atop of ye."

Preparations for winter, the housing of vegetables, cutting of wood, and the mowing of slough-grass for the cattle kept us so busy that we did not notice, one day in October, that the atmosphere was darkened by a huge black cloud. An organized band that night descended upon Hennepin county, determined upon rule or ruin. Each remaining vestige of verdure met destruction as it came in contact with the voracious mouth of one of these depredators. *Grasshoppers*, millions of them, swept over the land!

As we were not of that nation whose citizens nurture a fondness for frogs, grasshoppers and other fashionable fads, we realized that we could not live upon these insects — notwithstanding their fatness. I tried to save the cabbage by pouring salt all over and around the heads. The delighted grasshoppers so relished the vegetables with the addition of salt, that in the morning I could hardly find the stump of a stalk. I let them finish the garden without salt. Only a comparatively small portion of the land was cleared up, and the grasshoppers devoured almost our all.

I now traded my oxen off in order that I might have only my pony and cow to winter. A new town, named Smith Town, was laid out on a beautiful location about four miles from Excelsior, and I helped to survey the lots, and during the winter put up ice for the new families. The winter was very cold, and the ice was four feet in thickness. The sleighing was fine, and sleigh-bells jingled merrily during all the winter.

In the spring, when the snow melted, a melancholy sight met our eyes. The grasshoppers, the previous autumn, had deposited millions of eggs in the soil, and the outlook for raising a crop was depressingly unpromising.

About this time, Mr. Gideon offered me a fine team of horses and a carriage for five hundred dollars. Believing that the grasshoppers would for some time prevent all profit from farming, I offered him a hundred acres of land for the team (a horse and a mare) and the carriage. He accepted, and I deeded him one hundred acres of Hennepin county land. I had a good lumber-wagon, and I traded the carriage for a carryall, and was now prepared for teaming. There was no one in Excelsior to do this kind of work, and I regretted much that the proving up on my Forest Dale land, and enforced attendance upon a jury at Minneapolis, kept me away from home until the first of May. County funds were then very low, and I only received half pay for my services as juror.

Early on the morning of May 2, I harnessed my untried team, and with Pat Murphy started for Forest Dale with five hundred feet of lumber. In order to avoid going four miles around, I again decided to try the Narrows.

"What are you doing with that lumber?" asked Mr. Hull, the ferryman; "I can't ferry all of that over."

"I do not intend that you shall," I answered.

"Can your horses swim?"

"I think that they will be glad to swim when they get into the deep water," I replied.

"Can *you* swim?" he asked.

"I swam across the Serpentine and back, in the city of London," I answered.

"Pat can take the ferry-boat over," said Mr. Hull.

"He can ride one of the horses," I replied.

"No, thank you," answered Pat. "I think if Mr. Hull don't object, I'd as soon stay by the boat."

I now prepared to enter the stream, and Pat was so frightened that he stood in front of the team, urging me to go around by the other road.

"Stand aside!" I commanded.

Pat obeyed, and I touched "Charley," the noble horse, with the whip, and a few moments later we were climbing the steep bank on the opposite side. Pat swung his cap and followed. We had no trouble with the horses as with the oxen, and were congratulating ourselves upon this fact when we reached the tree once bearing the curious legend, "Turn, turn, accursed stranger, turn!" I was looking at the tree and wondering what freak of human nature had posted up this notice, when the horses suddenly began to sink, and to my horror kept going down into what must have been a bed of quicksand and mud.

"Pat!" I shouted, "do not come near me!"

The boy had been running along the ridge, and he came now to my aid, surprised and frightened; but I ordered him away. I did not wish him to be in any danger for my sake. Hastily jumping down from the wagon, up to my waist in mud and water, I loosened the horses. After hours, it seemed to me, I succeeded in getting the horses extricated, and Pat tied them up while I sat down to rest. While Pat ate his dinner, I meditated on the pleasant task before me of carrying the lumber from the wagon, and then getting it out; of the possible danger of the treacherous mud and quicksand, and the uncertainty of pioneer life. After much exertion I succeeded in unchaining the lumber and reaching it out to Pat, who received and carried it to dry land.

"Sure, Mr. Brake, are you going to leave the wagon?" asked Pat.

"Not I," I said. "Out it comes, if it takes a week."

"I'm thinkin'," said Pat, "it'll be rather lonesome loike for ye. Of course ye'll not expect me to kape company wid a single individual for a whole wake wid scant livin' for a single breakfast."

Morning dawned after a long and weary night. The horses were uneasy, and the attentions of bloodthirsty mosquitoes did not add to the general comfort. I began at once to tie the ropes and chains together, and fasten them to the tongue of the wagon. In a few moments, with the aid of the horses, the wagon came out of the mud and water and stood on dry land. The dark night, the wild animals that had made the hours hideous, our wet garments and unsatisfied hunger, were forgotten. My valuable team, wagon and lumber were saved. We were past the quicksand and water, and our way lay clear before us.

Once home again in safety, and my wife's anxiety at rest, I decided to try to earn some money with my team by running a hack from Excelsior to St. Paul. The depredations by grasshoppers rendered it necessary that I seek some means of subsistence.

It was now midsummer, and both myself and Charles Galpin, who also carried passengers, did a thriving business. The canoes obtained from the Indians were now in constant demand. Many invalids flocked to the new watering-places, Excelsior and Forest Dale, where, in the healthful pursuits of rowing and fishing, health came to them.

One of my passengers, a Mr. Lithgow, stayed in our neighborhood, secured a claim, and built him a cabin. He was a wealthy gentleman, and soon rigged up a sail-boat and spent much time upon the lake. One day, while thus occupied, a sudden gust of wind overturned the boat, and Mr. Lithgow was drowned. This, our first tragedy, caused a gloom to settle over the entire community.

Another passenger was a Congregational minister named Charles B. Sheldon. He was a good and able man, and remained with us and preached for us. He had a large family and his salary was small, but he managed by economy to make a living in the new country.

My wife accompanied me on one of these trips from St. Anthony, and a gentleman named Maxwell rode home with us. As we rode along, Mr. Maxwell said:

"Mr. Brake, if you will stop at Purgatory, I will furnish you with a load worth more than a thousand dollars."

"Purgatory must be a station from which passengers would like to travel even by a hack. I'll stop," I replied.

I knew that the place had been so nicknamed on account of the mud-hole in the road. Bridges and culverts being then unknown, we gave the rough places cheerful and expressive names. We reached the spot, and to our surprise were presented with the prettiest child I have ever seen. The family was poor, and the parents had several children. As our children had all died in infancy, believing we would be able to support little seven-year-old Lizzie better than they, she was offered to us as a gift. It would be impossible to express our gratitude. A thousand dollars, indeed! She seemed of value above calculation. And to this day the child, whose father died soon after, has been the crowning blessing of my life. Our hearts have been cemented in a bond of love that shall never be broken on this earth, nor yet in the world to come.

For some time after this, as though fortune had filled my cup sufficiently full, I did very little. I carried a good many people, but they were mostly prospective settlers whom I charged nothing. Interested in the town,

I hoped to reap a future reward when my passengers should have settled in Excelsior. Again, I carried goods free to our village of Forest Dale, and this took up much time. My boy, Pat Murphy, and my chopper, Charlie Herman, were doing little work, and, with the fast-approaching winter at hand, I resolved to remain at home a short time, not only to look after wood and feed, but to enjoy the society of my dear little daughter and her mother.

My time was so full that my pocket was empty before I knew it. As we kept open house to sojourners in our wilderness, we could not afford to be idle, so I started on a trip to St. Anthony, but found at Excelsior that my friendly competitor, being more of a smart Yankee than I, had picked up all of the trade. There was a half-way house between Excelsior and St. Paul, kept by a man who managed his brother while his brother managed the house. Very appropriately his name was Self. Two passengers paid the bill at Mr. Self's and I went on to St. Paul. After waiting a full hour, I was turning away in disgust when I was accosted by a stout German.

"So, Mr. Hackdriver, do you want a yob?"

Did I! "Yes," I exclaimed, "here I am for that purpose."

"I lif near Buffalo Lake, up the country," he said.

"I know the lake," I replied. "It is twenty-five miles away."

"I haf some few goods already," he said, "I do want you to haul."

"How much weight?" I asked.

"Fife barrel of flour, two sack of salt, fife hundred weight other goods — about von ton."

"Do you want to ride?" I asked.

"Nix," he answered, "I vos big enough to walk, und to help roll der wheels oop bad places, eh!"

"What are you willing to pay? It is a hard trip."

"Eh!" He took a ten-dollar gold piece from his pocket and held it up; "I gifs you this, und ten pound sausage."

The gold looked tempting. My purse needed replenishing. I was sure that my wife and Lizzie would enjoy the sausage. I accepted his offer.

It was a tiresome journey, but a little after dark we reached the place. I was so tired that I retired as soon as supper was eaten. When I arose in the morning I found myself in a commodious subterranean habitation, the front part of which was a small store, where, at an immense increase in price upon the cost, the goods I had carried would be retailed to customers. I wondered where the latter were to come from, for there was not a dwelling within miles of my German host. Neighbors, however, were not lacking, for my nostrils informed me that the relatives of the source of the sausages promised me were very near at hand.

Breakfast was soon ready. Brown bread, home-made and baked in a clay oven, coffee and fresh sausages soon made me forget the proximity of the pig-sty.

"I do put up some hog meat, too, already for your frau," the German lady said as she packed the sausage.

I inquired the road to Excelsior. My German friend replied:

"If you do go the long road it will be thirty mile; if you do go through, you safe fife mile. There is only one bad mud-hole; you can go through him *easy* already."

Such clear instruction was not to be disregarded. I decided to "go through him." Near the mud-hole named lived a settler. I asked him if he thought I could cross the place.

"Certainly," he said. "It's not a bad place."

I drove in accordingly, and in about the middle of the mess, the horses sank deeply in the mud.

"Come and help me," I cried; "Halloa! Halloa!"

The rare spectacle of a Minnesota pioneer refusing aid to another now presented itself. To my surprise he came and laughed at my predicament.

"Ten dollars would be a small sum, I reckon, stranger, to you. I make my livin' by this mud-hole. What'll you pay to get out?"

"You are an impostor!" I yelled.

"You'd better shoot them horses," he answered; "they're as good as dead now. I'll bring my oxen then and help you out. Hand over your X."

I jerked up my rifle.

"If I shoot anything, it will be you, you varmint!" I shouted.

He took me at my word, and vanished. I waded in, and by almost superhuman efforts loosened and backed the horses out upon dry land. Fastening a chain in the pin-hole and attaching it to the horses, they pulled the wagon out backward. I now patiently retraced my steps, and sadly took my way homeward by the "thirty-mile" road. As I had to stay all night at the Minnetonka mills, four days and nights had elapsed from the time of my departure when I reached home. My ten dollars in gold, and the fresh meat, hardly recompensed me for the anxiety of my wife, and the jaded condition of the team. Such were the experiences of hack-drivers in those early times.

My wife was taken very sick about this time, and as

usual I nursed her through her illness. All through the beautiful month of October, while Nature was donning her most gorgeous robes, and hundreds of visitors were enjoying the rare lake scenery, my wife lay at death's door. When she recovered she was so changed that an acquaintance would not have known her. She was emaciated to a skeleton, and her magnificent raven hair had fallen off. It was a long time before she recovered her usual health.

That fall our house was full of sufferers from sickness and hard times. A stout German whom I cured of eczema chopped wood for me all winter, and an ex-Catholic priest who had been driven away by Indians from a church he was building, put me up a house. An Englishman who lived in a cave changed it for our home, and I also gave him work. I certainly lost nothing through kindness to these people, for they did faithful work, even to one of Sir Walter Scott's heroines, who under the name of Lobsdale came to us for work at the carpenter business. Perhaps the priest may have been her friend; at any rate, her identity was so well concealed by her male attire that she had been gone some time before we learned who she was.

In the fall of 1856, money seemed to abound in and around Excelsior. The holders of this "wild-cat" currency bought up thousands of acres of land, to the ruin of the original claimants. But, perhaps in no year was Christmas more royally observed by the pioneers of Hennepin county than in 1856. Our own plum-pudding was as enjoyable as its predecessors. We still had our claim, our health, the blessing of appreciative friends, and the crisis even then just upon the horizon had not troubled us.

We ate our Christmas dinner with grateful hearts, and rejoiced in our surroundings.

In January, a gentleman named Russell living up the lake came and asked me to haul him some lumber.

"Is the ice safe?" I asked.

"Two feet thick," he replied. "I rode down here on a horse. The snow is not deep and it is not drifted. I need the lumber badly, and will pay you well for your work."

We now had a saw-mill at Excelsior. The order was upon the miller, Mr. Wilcox, for five hundred feet of lumber. On a bright, cold morning, I started to take the lumber to its destination. Unwilling to risk the strength of my horses, I borrowed a yoke of stout oxen, went to Excelsior and loaded the lumber, and went overland to the Narrows between the two lakes. The miller called after me as I drove away from the mill:

"Take a shovel along, and wrap up; you can't fool with forty degrees below zero."

The ice by this time was three feet thick; the only danger I could fear in crossing the lake was from the snow, which the icy wind was heaping into hills and scooping into hollows. It was worse at the edge. It took me an hour to clear a road wide enough for the sled. The smaller drifts in the way impeded my progress much, but at last the six miles were traversed, the lumber carried up the steep bank, and my oxen turned toward home.

It was sunset by this time, and night, with no moon, and only the snow and stars to lighten the darkness, soon fell around me. Wolves followed me so closely that I often took a stake from the sled and drove them back. Although I moved slowly and kept a constant lookout for my pathway so lately traveled, I soon found that I had missed my way, and knew not where I was. The anxiety of my family, the certainty of death from cold, to say nothing of the wolves, the drifts ahead of me, and my desire to return the cattle safely, combined to make me afraid to advance into unseen danger. But the peril was even worse if I stood still in the darkness, so I journeyed on, my feet frozen and my limbs almost numb with cold. I kept constantly kicking my feet against the sled, but as my faculties became deadened I found it difficult to keep up the effort. Bracing myself, however, I moved forward, and at last saw a faint light in the distance. That light saved my life. It proved to be from without the home of a Miss Johnson, who lived alone save for a small boy, and with whom I was well acquainted. Her house, before which a fire had been lighted to scare away wolves, was in an exactly opposite direction from my home. With difficulty I got the cattle up a steep bank, tied them to the sled, and went into the house.

Miss Johnson at once brought me some hot tea, and then prepared my supper. With tepid water I removed the bandages from my frozen feet, and after dressing them retired to the bed kindly prepared for me by the lady. In the morning I hobbled out, yoked up my oxen and started home. I met my hired man in a short time. He had found my dog, which had frozen to death, and had little hope of finding me alive until I came in sight.

The pain from my frozen feet was almost unsupportable. It was a month before I could resume work, and I looked about me for something that would help increase the small amount of money we had in reserve.

A Mr. Stevens built a small movable house, and we

moved it from point to point on the lake. He would then cut a small hole in the ice within the room, and build a little fire. The fish, attracted by the light, would come to the surface, and he would spear them. I made a great box and lined it with zinc. In this, upon my recovery, I carried large quantities of fish to St. Anthony, now my terminal point, where I sold them at the hotel. We did a paying business during the rest of the winter, Mr. Stevens spearing them as fast as I could sell them. Of course I carried other passengers besides the dead fish, and hauled many goods for the merchants at Excelsior.

On one of these trips, I stopped at Mr. Self's refreshment house, and he took me out to a fine open prairie to see one of the typical sights of civilization in its early contact with Indians. A tribe of these wild men had camped upon the prairie, and some vile miscreants, knowing the effect of liquor upon these children of Nature, hauled two barrels of whisky out upon the prairie and sold it to them. Once in possession of all of the money the Indians had, the whisky-sellers decamped and were soon out of the reach of the law. The scene on this, the following day, was terrible in the extreme. Old blankets, rags, butts of muskets, covered the ground. A large spot was red with human blood, and pieces of hoops and staves were covered with blood and human flesh. Squaws nearly nude, children, old men, and wounded and disabled (some of them scalped) warriors groaned and wept at being left to care for each other or die. The poor drunken wretches had drank the vile, poisonous stuff until they were infuriated, and then fought each other until dead, disabled, or sober; after which, those who could travel had gone off, and left their helpless friends to their fate.

After such a scene, and the danger that would have resulted to a white man if alone he had met the fleeing braves, home and the society of my wife and dear little girl seemed doubly precious. The Sabbath service and Reverend Charles B. Sheldon's able sermon had more of a tranquilizing effect upon my mind than those of any previous occasion.

But however sweet home might be, our daily bread had to be earned.

On the next trip, on my return, the ice on the lake began to break up — and such a tearing, rending, roaring, crackling sound I have never heard. It was like the voice of many thunders. As it was after dark, I dismounted from my seat and examined the ice. It was not yet broken, but the subterranean noises, the constant vibration, warned me that I might expect a rent at any time. Sure enough, a little farther on the ice suddenly shook, yawned, and with a terrible explosion a chasm was formed directly under the horses' feet. The cold waters bubbled up rapidly, and the animals were almost unmanageable. Fortunately, I got them across the narrow gulf, and at a rate of speed hardly attained by modern turf trotters my horses spun over the creaking, swaying ice to Brake's Landing, where my hired man, his teeth chattering with fear and cold, was waiting for me.

The next day I went up to Forest Dale to see about my land. Not wishing to risk the lake by night, upon returning, I sent Pat Murphy, who had accompanied me, home with a friend, Mr. Langdon; and my neighbor, Mr. Latterner, a tailor, rode with me in the sled. We kept as near the shore as possible, and in order to do so rounded the points of land jutting out into the water. Passing around one of these, we came near a spring, and the mare suddenly sank to her collar in water. I soon drew my noble horse "Charley" on safe ice, but the water froze upon me as fast as I stepped out of it. I was very cold. I tried to get the mare out, but finding that I could not, and hearing the sound of axes, I left her turning around in the hole, and mounting "Charley," rode off toward the noise of the logging-camp. Looking back, I could see her head moving in her attempts to get out. The two miles to the camp seemed a long distance, but at last the three men, with cattle and chains, were on their way toward my sled, and a few minutes later, to my great joy, I saw shining in the air the bright shoes of the mare as she plunged upon the ice.

There was a house in the woods, and Mr. Latterner had gone there and changed his foot-gear while we were extricating the mare. My poor horses, covered with ice and trembling with cold, were as presentable as I was in my glistening array, when Mr. Latterner, warm and dry, rejoined us. I had heard that it takes nine tailors to make a man. I now believed the story.

When I reached home, Pat was blubbering. He had been there a long time; it was past midnight, and all were wondering what had become of Mr. Latterner and myself.

"What is the matter, Pat?" I inquired.

"Sure," said Pat, "I was so cold and tired. I only wanted to rest a bit by the way, and Mister Langdon kicked and pounded me into a run. I'd never be kickin' a crayther that was smaller than meself. You, Mister Brake, are not so big as I be, but never a toime did I kick and pound ye."

Mr. Langdon laughed. "Pat tells the truth," he said; "I had to scare him into a run with a stick, and then make him believe I was after him all the way home, to keep him from going to sleep and freezing to death."

"I reckon," said Pat, reflectively, "that half a skin is better than none. If it's dead on the road I was about to be, and I've escaped with me loife, I'll hold no spite at Mister Langdon. Only sometoime I'll return the compliment, and save him from freezin' in as gallant a manner as he saved me. Then I'll feel sure enough loike a hero."

My wife clung to me when I had told my story, weeping bitterly at the danger through which Pat and I had passed. Notwithstanding the fact that I ate heartier than ever before, she persisted in looking upon me as though I had been dead and was alive again, and as though she was sure it was myself and not the mare that had so narrowly escaped death.

"How long must I endure these fears for your safety? When will these uncertainties, anxieties and forebodings cease? It is hastening me into insanity. Do let us leave this terrible lake country, and put an end to this interminable trouble and worry."

I tried to comfort her, but the long-pent lava of emotion had burst forth in a very torrent of words, and she would not be soothed.

"The crisis so long talked about and dreaded is here," she cried. "I can see that you are making no money. Your thousands brought from New York are almost gone, your five-hundred-dollar team nearly worthless. Your life is in constant jeopardy, and I am a slave, mentally and physically, to this wretched life. Take me out of this place. I cannot stand this life any longer. Do, please do, say it shall be ended!"

I was overcome by the vehemence of Charlotte's emotion, and acquiesced in her wishes.

"This year shall wind up my affairs in Minnesota Territory," I answered. "My dear, you shall have your way."

And so, as is frequently the case with other men, my wife changed the whole tenor of my future life. After mature deliberation, my wife consented to remain until the fall of 1858, and I set to work to complete the logging, lumber, and other contracts I had on hand, preparatory to removing from the Territory.

By summer, the crisis, as my wife had stated, had reached us. Business was at a standstill. Forest Dale was not improving. Excelsior was dead to improvement. A quarter-section of land would not have brought fifty dollars. The wild-cat money was not fit for pipe-lighters, and I had enough of the stuff to make me lose heavily. I turned my attention to putting in my small crop, and my resolve to please my wife, and leave the Territory, was daily strengthened by her entreaties.

Lizzie was now a thriving, cheerful little girl, eight years of age. We sent her to the Excelsior school, where she learned rapidly. She came running to meet me always upon my return, and her presence in these trying times was a constant inspiration. I resolved that we should have a little pleasure during the rest of our stay in Hennepin county; so I rigged up a row-boat, and we all went each evening with rod and reel upon the lake. We caught more fish than we could use. We made us a garden, and, despite the crisis, we planted and enjoyed not only vegetables, but flowers. I raised a crop, and we were all happy together, for a short time at least, in the new Territory.

During the summer, I started to take a Mr. Payson to his claim. The distance being about forty miles, and the mud in places to the knees of the single horse we drove, it took a week for the trip. We slept in a clayey swamp one night; in a great forest the next. The horrors of the last night were beyond comparison with Indians, wolves, ice, or cold. My mother's prophecy concerning the trunks of mosquitoes seemed verified. I climbed a tree and hid in the branches, but my companion could not climb, and his moans and cries would have made a passer-by believe he was being murdered. In the morning we were covered with our own blood. Those mosquitoes must indeed have been thirsty for gore. We thought it likely that the ghosts of departed Indians were resenting our intrusion upon their domain, and if so, they certainly early drove us off the premises. We reached the land office, where Mr. Payson proved up on his claim, after which, upon our return, we took a longer way around, thus avoiding the waiting weapons of the carnivorous mosquitoes.

The fall days passed rapidly; the swamp-grass was mowed and put up for hay; the small products of our clearing gathered for the winter, and I again looked for work for my team. In hauling a heavy load of shingles for our Episcopalian minister, Dr. Chamberlain, I broke down my wagon, and, until I could get another, loaned and hired out my horses.

Mr. Hull, the ferryman, first had "Charley" for use. The noble animal was turned into Mr. Hull's pasture across Lake Minnetonka. In the morning, when Mr. Hull came to tell me that "Charley" was either strayed or stolen, I took him to the stable. Clean and dry, beautiful as a picture, the faithful creature stood in his stall. He had swum the lake!

I next hired the team to a laborer named Christian Biblizen, near Buffalo Lake. He was to pay me if any damage accrued to the horses, but it was with sad misgivings I saw them go. Still, they must help with our living, and the twenty dollars offered for their use was not to be refused. My forebodings were realized. On the way home, Mr. Biblizen got into a floating swamp. The horse was saved, but the mare sank entirely out of sight. I never saw the creature again. I received a note for fifty dollars for the loss. It is still in my possession, and unpaid.

There was not much chance now to get away. My money was spent, my team broken. I made a pair of shafts and put them in my hack, hoping that "Charley" would in some measure fill the place of the two horses. Minneapolis was now becoming quite a little town, and I found some work, not only in carrying my usual accompaniment of goods and passengers, but in the sale of fish. The prospects for this business were better than ever before. By Christmas Day, 1857, the lake was safely frozen over, and Mr. Stevens could begin spearing fish. So our prospects for the winter were fair enough to permit us to enjoy the cheer of this to us double anniversary day. Judge McLeod came down from the shores of Lake Superior to spend the day with us, and meet a merry company of friends. Doctor, surveyor, engineer, merchant and farmers gathered around the board that day, and told tales of Philadelphia, of Boston, of New York, and of that more modern yet not less wonderful city — St.

Paul. The snow was deep, and for ten days the sleigh-bells rang, and hospitable doors stood open to the visitors who came in sleighs to visit the cheery friends near Excelsior.

The immigration into the Territory of Minnesota at this time was remarkable. On February 26, 1857, Congress had passed an enabling act for its admission into the Union, and on May 11, 1858, Minnesota became a State. As early as 1843, the Indian title to the lands east of the Mississippi had been extinguished, and in 1851 the titles west of the Mississippi met the same fate. Hence there was an abundance of land now open to settlement, which, with the healthful climate, caused hundreds and thousands to seek homes in the embryo State. Minneapolis, founded in 1849, but containing only one family in 1852, was growing rapidly, although it gave little promise of the great city it was afterwards to become.

To the sturdy Swiss settlers near St. Paul had been added many others, and Stillwater was coming into importance as a town. There was now going on a great rush for homes.

It will be seen that I had lost my mare just when the business of teaming would have become a paying one. But the large influx of settlers made the fish business profitable, and I carried it on throughout the winter.

In February I found my stock without feed, and left home to procure some corn or oats. As there were many cattle dying from starvation and exposure in the surrounding country, I bought some hides, thinking that I could exchange them for corn in St. Paul. Within four miles of home my sled broke down. There was nothing to be done but leave my load of corn and hides, go home, make a new runner, and return. I had with me a valuable dog. I told him to get on the hides and stay there until I told him to get off, and not let anyone touch the skins. The dog obeyed me, for upon my coming back, forty-eight hours later, he was still at his post. I made a new runner and took the sled back, and hauled the hides to St. Paul. I forgot to call the dog when I started home. Two weeks later the man who had bought the skins stopped me on the streets of St. Paul, and said:

"For Heaven's sake, come and call off your dog! All the feeding and coaxing I can do will not get him off the pile of skins. He would eat me up, I believe, if I touched them."

I had thought that the dog was lost. Instead of following me, however, he had waited for permission to leave his charge. I coaxed him out and took him home.

On February 25th, 1858, occurred one of the most terrible blizzards I have ever witnessed. Mr. Latterner and myself had gone from Excelsior to St. Anthony on business, and had proceeded as far as the center of Crystal Lake before the storm struck us. We could not see a rod ahead of us. The icy wind swept the lake, chilling us through, and the snow drifted so rapidly we could not find our way. Foolishly enough, I took the guidance instead of trusting to the instinct of my horse, and in a few moments we were entirely at fault. After circumnavigating the lake we were still unable to tell which way would give us shelter. But now I stopped "Charley," let him look about him, and take his own way. In a moment he gave a great snort and sprang up a steep bank, and when he paused we were on the road to Minneapolis. The noble creature had saved our lives. We were frightfully cold. Mr. Latterner said:

"If we only had some spirits along, they would keep us from freezing."

"I have a small flask," I answered, "if I could get at it."

"For God's sake!" he cried, "find it. I am surely falling asleep from the cold."

We certainly were freezing.

"Hold the lines!" I shouted, for he seemed about to faint.

Fumbling about with my numb fingers, I at last produced the flask and gave it to him.

"It is a lump of ice," he said in despair.

"Put it near the fire," I said, "when you get to Minneapolis. Dry whisky is the best in a blizzard."

"Don't talk of fire here!" he cried, angrily; "how can you joke at such a time?"

But his firing up kept him awake until he had managed to get a few drops of the liquor into his throat. Being of a phlegmatic temperament, whisky elevated him. It would have depressed me.

We reached Mr. Bertram's home in Minneapolis at last, and found the family absent. As they were not expecting us, and might be gone some time, we entered and took possession. The red-hot stove and the well-filled larder made us quite comfortable until the return of the family. We did not stand on ceremony. As the strong man armed was not keeping his palace, he need not expect that his goods should be in peace. However, the Bertrams atoned for their absence upon their return, by increased attention to our comfort.

When I started home, the blizzard was not only over,

and the sun shining bright, but it had turned warm, and there had set in a thaw. Before I reached Lake Crystal, Mr. Latterner having gone on to St. Paul, my horse was plowing his way through mud.

It was the Sabbath day, and, as if to punish me for violating the ordinance concerning it, my cutter broke down, and it was late in the night when "Charley" and I reached home. As I fixed up a clumsy makeshift for my runner, I had time enough to reflect upon my Christian duty, to resolve to fulfill my wife's wishes and leave this pioneer life, as well as to be a better man. She had no difficulty in inducing me to promise that night that no matter what should transpire I would make this year the last which should witness the dangerous adventures incumbent upon a citizen of this new Territory.

So, I began to make everything bend to this result. Dismissing Pat, I gave my own personal attention to my crop, and for three months remained at home, busy with my farming. From June to September I resumed my hack-driving to St. Paul and Minneapolis. No such harvest had blessed my efforts at farming since I had been in the Territory. On my small clearing I had five hundred heads of cabbage, not one of which would have gone into a bushel basket. Two hundred bushels of fine Irish potatoes and a hundred dollars' worth of corn for sale; loads of melons and pumpkins and all other vegetables in proportion, promised me the means in the near future to leave for a more thickly-settled country. I began to regret having to leave this fruitful land for others unknown to me; but our minds were decided, and we began our preparations for departure.

Money was scarce now, and times hard; hundreds of

dollars due me were unpaid, and could not be collected. There was little sale for anything. I traded my corn for lots in Excelsior, sold my faithful "Charley" to Mr. Sheldon, left my vegetables and furniture in the hands of a supposed trustworthy friend, and with my family went down to St. Paul for a boat.

I came to Excelsior with three thousand dollars. I left it with just ninety-nine dollars safe in the fold of my purse. I may as well say here, that with the exception of some money afterwards paid me by Mr. Sheldon, I never received either property or money from Excelsior. A report that we had been murdered by Indians had something to do with the neglect or failure of persons interested in sending us our just dues.

As I passed through Excelsior, I realized, however, that my work as a pioneer had not been in vain. When we landed on the lake-shore in 1852, the surrounding region was a wilderness, undisturbed save by the steps and voices of red men. Wild beasts infested the forests, and civilization seemed afar off. Now, the country was being transformed into a fertile farming community; where I had built the first white man's cabin six years previous, Excelsior, a thriving village, now stood. A church, school-house, hotel, dry goods and merchandise stores and a post-office were here, and fifty-five persons might be counted as residents. Since Excelsior has become a famous watering-place, reached half a dozen times a day by cars from Minneapolis and St. Paul, I have never seen it. With its beautiful homes in which reside eminent physicians and retired merchants, I am not familiar. I have never looked upon its excellent college, nor seen its splendid green-houses and market gardens, nor yet watched steamers sailing away from its piers. But the Excelsior of that autumn day, when I last looked upon it, and upon the faces of the concourse of kind and affectionate friends who had come to see us off, will remain vividly in my mind so long as life shall last. We looked about us at the prospects, since fulfilled, of a great agricultural region; we inhaled the fresh breeze of Minnetonka, and looked upon the gorgeously tinted forests, and were sorry to go. Yet Providence dealt wisely with us. The details of the horrible Indian massacre of 1861, which took place only a few miles from our home, would have forever shattered my poor wife's nervous system. She could never hear of the two hundred slain women, of the decapitated babes, of the trees spattered with human blood and brains, without convulsive shudders of horror. It was well we missed a more perfect knowledge of all this, by leaving while we had the means to remove to another Territory.

"Charley," who remained in Mr. Sheldon's charge until death, as beloved by every person in the neighborhood as an intelligent child would have been, carried us through water and mud to St. Paul. I have sometimes wondered if this faithful horse in his subsequent life,—for he was twenty-five years old when he died—remembered the master who more than once owed life itself to his sagacity.

Never on earth shall I see the friends who stood on the bank that November day to witness our departure on the last boat of the season, but the day of our reunion is not far distant. I shall meet them in the life beyond. Dr. Sellers, who with his family had spent a winter in my home; Judge McLeod, whose love was like a brother's; Captain Locke, of the Fort, Mr. Morris and Mr. Bokee (engineers), and many other dear friends who had shared our hospitality, grasped our hands at parting, and mingled their regrets with our own at the life-long separation before us.

The river was covered with a coating of ice, through which our boat plowed its way. By the time Lake Pepin was reached, the ice was over an inch thick. We reached St. Louis, however, in ten days, and put up at a hotel.

CHAPTER VII.

MISSOURIAN EXPECTATIONS.

Boat-fare was much cheaper in those days than are railroad tickets now. Our passage, including board, only cost us fourteen dollars. The trip was a pleasant one and it was with great satisfaction that I listened often to glowing praises of St. Paul, Minneapolis, Stillwater, and Excelsior —all towns of which I was justly proud.

After a days' rest with my family, I carried my letter of introduction from Reverend Mr. Chamberlain to Dr. Berkely, of the Episcopalian church, and sought by his assistance to find work ere my ninety-nine dollars escaped into the cold. I rented a small two-roomed house, bought a stove and a box or two, and we went to housekeeping. In this strange city, we had no friends. The luxury of a two-roomed house was evidently sufficient for a family fresh from the wilds of Minnesota, for no person extended to us a helping hand. After two months, I at last secured a position as dairyman for a man who had a ranch in New Mexico. I was too nearly without means to refuse any situation offered me, but, as the expedition would not start until February, I had to do something until then. So I secured a temporary home for Lizzie, my wife engaged her services as nurse to an invalid lady, and I worked as waiter in the hotel at the ferry-boat landing at St. Charles.

The immense bridge which spans the Mississippi at St. Louis was only a dream in 1858, and the cars of the Iron

Mountain Railroad were ferried across at St. Charles, Missouri; then, only a boarding-house.

I soon found that my Missourian hopes were groundless. There was nothing in St. Louis or vicinity for me. As the time drew near for my departure to New Mexico, I left St. Charles, went down to St. Louis, and bade my loved ones good-bye. The dangers of the journey were obvious enough to my own mind, but I tried to leave as favorable an impression of it as possible with my wife. The mother of Mr. Aleandro, or "Aley," as we called him, was blind. To her the way seemed full of perils, and she earnestly besought me to take care of her comfort and stay in her old age — her beloved son. Although I was strong and hopeful, I was not sure but my wife would have preferred the same request of Mr. Aley concerning myself if she had seen him. In those days the women dreaded, worse than death, the perils of the Western trails.

We were to ascend the Missouri river to Independence, go from there to Westport, Missouri, and on across the plains to New Mexico. We accordingly took the train for Jefferson City, and caught a boat there in the night for Independence.

Imagine our feelings when the boat, within eighteen miles of our destination, stuck in the ice, and no amount of pressure could budge it an inch farther. Worse than that, the captain put up placards all over the boat as follows:

"FIVE DOLLARS PER DAY
FOR ALL PASSENGERS STAYING ON THIS BOAT."

There was nothing else to do but disembark. The "passengers" went ashore, secured a farm wagon as a conveyance, a farmer as a driver, and jolted into Independence about midnight. As for myself, I was so cold that I put my small luggage on my back, and walked most of the way. In the morning, we went on to Westport, where Mr. A. had a fine span of American mules. The next day we left for Council Grove, Kansas, the rendezvous of freighters and traders who were crossing the plains. Kansas City stands now near the old town of Westport, but, save for the Wyandotte Indians, there were few settlers then on this side of the river.

CHAPTER VIII.

A TRIP ACROSS THE PLAINS.

We started February 1, 1858, Mr. A. and myself driving his mules to a buggy. We made half of the one hundred and forty miles the first day, sleeping at night with a settler named Barricklow. Only a shell of a house, the building was barely inclosed, and I suffered greatly from cold. After an almost sleepless night, I arose and went out to see after the mules. My teeth were already chattering with cold, and I did not speak to the animals as I passed behind them with a bucket of water. One of them kicked at me, missed me, but hit the bucket, and sent the icy water in a shower-bath all over me. As the freezing liquid splashed in my face, ran around my neck and down my spinal column, my initiation into the mysteries of freighting seemed complete.

Our fare settled, and the broken bucket paid for, we left this comfortable mansion. On the way to Council Grove, at the present Burlingame, Mr. A. employed a man named Louis Boyse to accompany us across the plains. We reached Council Grove that night, and began our arrangements for the trip to New Mexico.

Seth Hayes, so well-known as the first trader in the present county of Morris, Kansas, kept a store and an outfitting station at Council Grove at this time. He had in keeping now six small Mexican mules, a good pony, a large wagon, and various other necessary acquisitions to our outfit. It took us four days to get the animals ready and lay in a supply of everything needful for our journey. An old negress who worked for Mr. Hayes roasted coffee, made cakes, and gave us a keg of pickles and sauerkraut as relishes.

On the last night before we started, the prospect seemed especially gloomy to me. Far away from my wife and child, and six hundred miles of constant danger in an uninhabited region was not a pleasant prospect for contemplation. But I laughed with the rest, joked about roasting our bacon with buffalo chips, and the enjoyment we would derive from the company of skeletons that would strew our pathway.

The few business houses at this time were mostly log cabins, and there was very little attempt made by the citizens to follow the fashions; but there were dudes even then in Council Grove. One of these was not attired in a faultless broadcloth suit with buttonhole bouquet, eyeglass, and cane, but wore an elaborately trimmed buckskin suit fringed down the side. His attire was finished off with beaded moccasins — the artistic production of some Cheyenne squaw whose cunning hand had cut them "bias" at the toe and fringed them at the heel. He wore a broad-brimmed hat, and under it were heavy masses of unkempt hair. Upon either side of him hung a navy revolver, and a bowie-knife was stuck in his belt. He rode a richly-caparisoned mustang, and far surpassed the modern dude in appearance.

Amusement was not lacking, however, even at this early time. Besides the cowboys, there were the courts to furnish fun for the citizens, and even visitors or chance stayers in Council Grove had the stories of the time rehearsed for their amusement. I remember some of these stories caused much laughter as we sat listening to them around Mr. Hayes's fire.

A 'Squire Mansfield, then a squatter on the present site of Council Grove, tried a fellow for some misdemeanor, and he was found guilty. With much dignity the court sentenced the prisoner in the following announcement:

"The court stands adjourned. The constable now will march the prisoner to the nearest wet-goods establishment, and see to it that he sets up the liquor for attorneys, witnesses, and spectators. Boys, fall in!"

Another case as amusing was also related: B. F. Perkins, a talented young lawyer, was attorney for the plaintiff and a Colonel Sanford for the defendant. After the arguments were finished, His Honor delivered the following charge to the jury:

"Gentlemen, you have heard the evidence in the case. You have also listened to the words of the learned counsel for both plaintiff and defendant. If you believe what the counsel for the plaintiff has told you, then you'll side for him; and if you believe what the counsel for the defendant stated, decide for him. But, gentlemen of the jury, if you are like me, and don't believe what either of them said, then I'll be darned if I know what you can do. Constable, take charge of the jury!"

We went off in grand style the next morning. The huge prairie-schooner was well filled. We took with us for planting and feeding half a ton of shelled corn. Besides this, we had Hungarian-grass seed, rifles, boxes of crackers, bacon and sugar, robes, blankets, and many other articles — about two tons in all. Louis Boyse, a great fellow, bigger than the mule he rode, and myself, a small man, armed with a "blacksnake" whip, and riding a small pony, were the attendants. Mr. A. drove the six Mexican mules, and the American mules were tied behind the wagon. On the first day we only reached Diamond Springs, about twenty miles from Council Grove, and there camped.

We allotted thirty miles per day as our limit of travel, and usually made fifteen of them before breakfast. We would then camp, spend two hours cooking our breakfast and resting our horses, after which we would go fifteen miles further and stop for the night. At the close of the second day, we reached Cow creek, the last and only place of refreshment between Council Grove and Fort Union, New Mexico. A man kept a whisky shanty here, and sold cheap liquor and dear oysters to travelers. Few passed his "house" without doing ample justice to both viands and spirits. At noon of our third day out, we wished the *ranchero* farewell, and as his dwelling disappeared in the distance behind us, we found ourselves upon the Santa Fé trail, away from civilization, our faces toward Fort Union.

That night we picketed our animals, fed them, secured everything, made a fire, cooked our bacon and coffee, and with the consoling reflection that we had no more wood, prepared for the night. Mr. A. slept in the wagon, and Louis Boyse and I rolled ourselves in blankets and lay down upon a buffalo-robe under the wagon and slept soundly until morning. We were hungry and dirty the next day when our fifteen miles were made, and as we had reached a small creek, we performed our ablutions, and admired ourselves as mirrored in the operation. Mr. A. complimented us upon our agility and cleanliness in preparing breakfast. Talk about the element named being next to godliness! The latter was a long way from freighters crossing the plains by the Santa Fé trail, if cleanliness was a condition of its nearness. The sand must have been as good as mustard, though, for we relished our late breakfast better than we ever had one eaten in a first-class hotel.

We made our usual afternoon drive of fifteen miles, turned out as on the previous night, cared for our stock, ate our suppers, and retired to our respective "apartments."

Two days later brought us to the Big Bend of the Arkansas river, where there were dangerous quicksands. We camped for the night, hoping that we would meet the mail outfit here and secure help in crossing. The wagon being heavily loaded, Mr. A. decided to relieve it by taking out half a dozen sacks of corn and hiding them. If we did not meet the mail until we were over the river, we would sell the corn to the mail-drivers at cost, as they were always glad of an opportunity to secure corn so far from civilization. The mail did not come, and we deposited the corn as directed in a low place near the river.

Mr. A. now mounted the pony, reconnoitered a little, and started to cross in a zigzag direction, in order to avoid the quicksands. We followed with the mules and wagon. The pony was hardly in the river until it nearly disappeared from sight. Of all the yelling, screeching and scolding I ever heard, those men did the best job! But their horrible din either conciliated the demon of the river, or else the mules understood their business, for one thing is certain — we crossed in safety.

"Don't you think you will need your lungs?" I asked, when we all stood panting on the other bank. "I have heard that down in New Mexico, lungs are considered essential to existence."

"Shut up!" growled Mr. A. "Mules always have to be frightened nearly to death or they will not cross the river."

I begged pardon in the London dialect.

I now rode my pony ahead of the team to the brow of the hill, and looked around me. Lo! Just beyond was the whole tribe of Kiowa Indians. Boyse turned pale, and I would have enjoyed the ice on Minnetonka better than my present situation. Mr. A. sung out, "See to your revolvers and knives! Don't be frightened."

We stopped the team and awaited the arrival of the Indians. It was a motley scene. There were chiefs, bucks, squaws, papooses, horses, ponies, robes, blankets, pots and kettles — all mixed up in a general "jamboree" of noise, commotion, odor, and color. They at once surrounded us. Being in a civil mood, they merely begged some powder and lead. We gave it to them, without first putting it in rifles, and attempted a further conquest of their savage hearts by opening boxes of sugar and crackers, and offering them a dainty repast.

In a few moments they moved southward, and we now toiled up the steep and sandy ascent, the poor mules panting and quivering from the exertion. I rode along on the pony, plying my whip in circles over their backs, and pitying the dumb brutes with all my heart. Looking back, I saw a squad of about thirty of the roughs of the tribe, both squaws and braves, with faces painted black, yellow and red, coming after us, I was sure for plunder. They immediately overtook us, and began to talk of robbing and killing us. We took no notice of them, and they accompanied us to the top of the sand-hills. Mr. A. could understand them, and he learned that they expected us to cook for them. They were told they could have some sugar and crackers. Accordingly, they disposed themselves in a circle on the ground. I got out a box of crackers, filled a washbowl with sugar, and waited upon the rascals. Delighted and satisfied with this rare feast of good things, they insisted on all of us lighting our pipes and smoking a pipe of peace together. The fumes of their "kinnikinic" did not deceive us. They meant mischief. Suddenly the biggest and ugliest of the bucks sprang up, and led the way to the supplies in our wagon. The rest followed him.

To be left without food and ammunition, or animals to carry us onward, two hundred miles from a human habitation, was far from pleasant. We resolved to sell our supplies dearly. As the first Indian set his foot upon our wagon-step, we made a simultaneous rush at them with drawn revolvers and flashing knives. Each of us dragged a rascal down, and I was about to stick my man when Mr. A. shook his head in a silent "No." The Indians were evidently unarmed, and the majority of them seemed to wait the action of their leaders. They saw we were going to defend our lives and our goods, and one of them sprang upon the tongue of the wagon, and laid his hand upon our rifles. Louis Boyse caught him and flung him upon his back. With an indescribable, guttural howl, the injured redskin crawled off, and closing around him, they all raised their war-whoop. Such a prolonged, relentless, blood-curdling yell as that unearthly, simultaneous shriek given by those thirty savage hoodlums, I had never heard. It was worse than the supposed cries of the condemned in the infernal regions. But with their accustomed respect for what they claim to possess in a marked degree — personal courage — they decided to yield us the victory, and retire from the field, which they did with much precipitation.

When the Indians were out of sight, I made a fire of buffalo chips, put the coffee on to boil, spread a blanket for a tablecloth on the lap of Mother Earth, and placed thereon some canned stuff in order to save time. (Blessings on the man or woman who first thought of canning eatables! The idea has kept many a traveler over the plains to Pike's Peak or Santa Fé from starvation.) We did not talk as much as usual around our hastily improvised table. Thoughts of home and loved ones, possible loss of life and property, suffering, or perhaps starvation on these arid plains if we escaped from the Indians, were some of the ideas that flitted through our minds.

As for myself, some way a garbled version of the affair was later carried to my wife, to Minnesota, and even to England. I was believed dead. Persons holding my property appropriated it to their own uses. My wife and child mourned for me as lost to them by death at the hands of the Indians. Yet while most of the friends who wept over my supposed decease are cold in death, I still live to write the story of that February day in 1859.

In about half an hour after the Indians left us, we were again on our way, moving as rapidly as possible. We had not gone two miles further until we met a band of Cheyenne warriors, in full war equipage. They were beautifully painted, and dressed in red. They carried long spears, bows and arrows, and paid no attention to us except to say "How!" A few miles further on, we met the mail. The men informed us that the Cheyennes were after the Kiowas, hence the rapid movements of both bands. We devoutly hoped that the artistically draped Cheyennes would overtake the picturesque Kiowas, and make them repent of having gorged our sugar and crackers! The mail-drivers assured us of their pleasure in getting the corn awaiting them, and that the rest of our way was free from danger. We were more cheerful after that news was imparted.

The little mules were now stiff from so much stopping, and Mr. A. ordered me to use the whip more freely. The Indians had mocked my driving performances that morning, and the memory of it, along with other insults they had offered, made the poor little mules suffer, I am afraid, for I took a sort of revenge by cracking my whip at them, in the absence of the burly braves whom I longed to punish in like manner. We made twenty miles further before dark, then turned out, picketed our animals, cooked our suppers over our smoky chip fire, and early retired to rest.

The air was becoming remarkably mild by this time. Travel, relieved from the fear of Indians, was delightful. We even thought of amusement. When we had traveled about ten miles the next day, I said:

"I wish we had some fresh meat."

"I have a good rifle," said Mr. A., "and I am a sure shot. Do you like prairie dog?"

"It depends upon who cooks it," I answered.

"You shall cook it," replied Mr. A.

We were passing through a prairie-dog village. At the door of his habitation, a fierce young dog set up a yelp of remonstrance at our interrupting their councils, and Mr. A. silenced him with a bullet. Throwing the dog into the wagon, we went on to our limit of fifteen miles, and stopped for breakfast.

I had cooked 'possum, 'coon, even terrapin, in my time, and was not to be deterred by jeers from preparing fresh meat simply because there was no material at hand to cook but a prairie dog, and no fuel for a fire but buffalo chips. So I made my fire, put a vessel of water on to boil, and dressed the dog. A savory stew was soon prepared which threw fried bacon into the shade. All of us pronounced prairie dog superior to squirrel or rabbit, and declared that after this we would often have fresh meat.

We were near Pawnee Fork when we camped that night. After a good night's rest, undisturbed by dogged dreams or other reminders of our stew, we rose early, cleaned and greased our wagon-axles, and resumed our journey. We looked back at the sparkling water of the Ornado with regret. Before us lay a journey of fifty miles before we could hope to strike another plentiful supply of water. I wondered, too, if the breezes that swept this high table-land could speak, what tales of snow-storms, of sand-storms, of freezing and starving cattle, of perishing men, it would whisper in our ears.

We carried with us from our camping-place a supply of fresh water, and without breakfasting, made twenty miles. By this time we were again hungry for fresh meat. Mr. A. shot a fat young prairie dog as before, and I skinned the animal and prepared him for the pot. Being very lean myself, I have always been a great admirer of fat, and I testified to this admiration now by putting a piece of the stuff into my mouth. I had no more than masticated and swallowed that piece of fat until I was sicker than words can express. In disgust, I threw the whole dog away, and I have never since particularly cared for prairie-dog meat. As to the fat, that mouthful has lasted me through all of the years that have since elapsed. It took a strong cup of coffee to cure the dog fit from which we all seemed to be suffering, and bacon and eggs tasted like ambrosia. Louis laughed heartily, and insisted that I was attacked with hydrophobia; and Mr. A. said:

"You shall have an antelope in a day or two for your mess."

Never shall I forget the quantities of bleached bones upon the Ornado table-land! Tons of iron strewed the road, remnants of scenes when for temporary relief freezing men burned the woodwork of their wagons. Gloomy reflections would force themselves upon our minds when, almost without water, we camped for the night. But we were only ten miles from a fresh supply, and two or three hours' travel the next morning brought us to some beautiful springs. The earth was frozen around them, but the springs were open, and never had water seemed to us so delicious or precious.

Mr. A. declared we were now within the range of antelope, and as we approached the Cimarron river we caught several glimpses of these shy and beautiful animals. As we neared our camping-ground, he was fortunate enough to bring down a fine young kid. When we had camped for breakfast, we took a sack of buffalo chips — carried forward for fuel — made our fire, and for the first time in my life I had the satisfaction of cooking and helping to eat fried antelope-chops.

I had now ridden my pony three hundred miles: to say I was sick of riding, feebly expresses my feelings. I had been compelled to crack my whip at the poor little mules, too, until my shoulders were very lame. Some way or other, that was not all of my misery. The ghost of that antelope or some other mysterious influence affected me almost to tears. Suddenly I stopped the train. I could carry my vague regrets no farther. I must do penance for my sins. To my surprise, my companions were similarly affected. I said, languidly, "It is a good thing to be mutually agreed," and it was some minutes before my emotion or vomition would let me say more. When we had made our day's journey and stopped for the night, there were few words spoken. Nervous sympathy made words unnecessary. All we wanted was repose. We rolled up in our blankets in silence and fell asleep. Antelopes, graceful and fleet, flitted swiftly through my dreams; but I was as shy of them as they were of me.

For the first time during our journey, we stopped the next morning long enough to cook an early breakfast. I made some biscuits and some coffee. We partook sparingly, however; the lesson on intemperance had been too strongly impressed and expressed for us to fall again so soon.

We crossed the Cimarron that night, and drank a cup of tea on the opposite bank. Wrapped in our blankets, we lay down as usual to sleep, but something kept me awake: I did not know but what it might be prairie dog or antelope. Louis was the sleepiest-headed of mortals. Once asleep, nothing short of an earthquake would have disturbed him. As I slept lightly, and wakened easily, I always kept my boots and my only pony-bridle under my head, in order that I might be prepared for any emergency that might arise. I had just fallen asleep, when I felt something move under my head. I put up my hand: one of the boots and the bridle were gone. I sprang up in time to see in the dim light, the outline of a large wolf, but the yell I gave must have disconcerted his wolfship, for he ran, leaving the boot and the bridle. My companion knew nothing of it the next morning, and but for the condition of my property would have kept on insisting that it was all "a bootless dream." I had no fancy, however, to ride into Fort Union on a pony wearing a rope bridle, myself minus one boot, and I praised the fates that I had recovered my confiscated goods.

In two days from that time, without accident or incident, we had made sixty-five miles, and camped at the Rabbit Ear creek. A solitary Indian came up to us and warned us that there was trouble among the Utes, but we were more suspicious of him than of them, and watched him all night. We also met a second mail party here, and they reported the road clear. The climate was becoming very delightful, and when we had rested our mules, cleaned our wagon-axles, and bathed ourselves, we felt anxious to push forward to the next camping-ground, known to travelers by the trail name, "the Wagon Mound." It was about fifty miles to this point, and there was an abundance of water there, entirely free from alkali.

Often now small herds of antelope, evidently surprised at the invasion of their territory, lifted their pretty heads, and stared at us with their lovely dark eyes, scarcely moving from their tracks.

Mr. A., who was exceedingly fond of displaying his seventy-five-dollar rifle, at last called a halt, and looked knowingly at me.

"By all means," I said, answering the inquiry.

Mr. A. accordingly shot one of the beautiful creatures,

and that day when we halted we turned our backs upon our past experience, and dined on antelope.

The road here was a fine example of what Nature could display in the matter of irregularities on the earth's surface. The noise and turmoil incident to getting the mules over this tract of rough country either digested our supper or else our theories of temperance better accorded with our practice, for this time we suffered no inconvenience, and slept soundly during the night.

The next stopping-place was known to freighters by the elegant name of "The Devil's Backbone," and for this classical retreat we started while the morning star was yet visible. "Start the mules briskly," commanded Mr. A., "and keep them on the swing. If they are not kept warm they will cave in." So I plied my whip unmercifully. The big mules were very lame, and the little ones were in a pitiable condition. As for myself, I was no longer sick from riding — I was sore. Language cannot express my pity for the faithful dumb brutes, nor my own sufferings in my attempts to maintain a dignified position upon the pony. After three hours of rapid travel we camped, and made the wretched animals as comfortable as possible.

We were out of flour; so we soaked crackers and fried them, to eat with our slices of antelope, and then lay down and rested for two hours. Within ten miles of the "Devil's Backbone," a terrible wind- and sand-storm struck us. The sand not only filled our eyes, but all the air. We could not see each other or the mules. The latter were so frightened that we could hardly manage them, and they absolutely refused to advance. What would be the result should the storm continue any length of time, we could not foresee. It was impossible to cook, for we were without water; the darkness was most intense, and the terrific storm increased in violence each moment. We made the animals as safe as possible, and retired, cold and hungry, in a state of nervous depression impossible to describe.

But the storm did not last half the night. In the morning, all was safe, and the air was as fresh and balmy as in early spring-time. Our cheerfulness revived as we surveyed the heaped-up sand-drifts, and thought of the pleasure of plowing through them. But while we hitched up the mules I was thinking of the vicinity of the "Devil's Backbone," and asking myself if the proximity of Satan accounted for the sand being flung in our eyes and strewn in our pathway. The word "backbone" sent me off on another train of thought. We would emulate Job's patience, and travel on to a place of safety beyond the limits of his Satanic territory.

We traveled slowly now, for we were all nearly worn out, but we were certain if nothing happened, to reach Fort Union in three or four days. There were plenty of watering-places during these last stages of our journey. Point Rocks, Cold Springs and Wet Stone Basin were all passed, and with animals that had made better time than the mail — for we were only twenty-eight days on the road, including our delays on the Missouri river, at Independence, and Council Grove — we entered Fort Union March 1, 1859.

CHAPTER IX.

LIFE IN NEW MEXICO.

The day after our arrival in Fort Union, New Mexico, I was escorted to my new home, which was on a ranch belonging to Don Aleandro, on the Mora road, about eight miles from Fort Union and ten miles from the chief town, Mora.

Mr. A., being busy with his sutlership duties, commissioned a negro slave belonging to him to take the big mules and conduct me to the ranch. This man was in charge of five hundred head of cattle, and had come into the Fort for provisions. A mile from the ranch was an elevation he called "the mountain." I named it, "Mizpah." The appearance of the region before me from this elevation was unique. There was something in it both Spanish and beautiful. Glancing over the landscape, my eye fell upon a heap of stones surmounted by a cross.

"What does that mean, Jim?" I asked.

"That was a Mexican there buried," he replied. "Gambled — quarreled — got killed. We put him a cross; the *padre* order it. I know, señor, who done killed him. Don't you believe he's far away from you, señor."

It was not difficult to recognize the character of this man with whom I was afterwards obliged to have dealings.

I looked toward the house as we neared the ranch, and again paused to take a view of the surroundings. Although the nearest one was twenty miles away, and it would have taken a good fifty miles to reach most of them, the mountains looked very near, and seemed to form a semi-circle around the upper part of the ranch — a body of land four miles square. The River Mora formed a junction upon it with the Rio Coyote, and the graceful curves of these streams were encircled with copses of cedar, pine, and other evergreens, making it always seem perpetual summer. The land was irrigated, and was evidently very fertile. In the center of this tract of about two hundred acres was a massive adobe mansion, evidently very old, and of peculiar construction. Upon entering it I found it to contain a large number of rooms, including what was called a cook-house, and a fandango-room fifteen feet wide and fifty feet long, and a refreshment-room twelve by fifteen feet. At the back of the house were three large rooms with a door for egress into the yard. From this door at any time of day could be seen the snow-topped mountains. Opposite these were three large interior rooms for storing provender for man and beast. The front doors were large enough to admit carriages or wagons, and were heavily ironed. Inside of them were smaller doors, to be used for persons passing in and out. The woodwork of the back doors was filled with heavy-headed spikes, and although there were many windows *inside* the inclosure, there were none on the outside. Around the building was a great corral that would have held five hundred cattle or five thousand sheep. The wall was built of heavy pine logs set perpendicularly, in trenches three feet deep. A dozen peon houses flanked the outer part of the corral at the river side. The building, the plaza and the corral formed a fort as it were, almost impregnable to Indians.

Jim pointed out the various rooms and their uses. The

great kitchen had a huge fireplace furnished with shelves for the roasting of whole calves or sheep, and it had an opening in one side to pass the viands into the refreshment-room, and also into the best room of the "miadoma" and his family. Across the hall was a large room for visitors attending the Mexican fandangoes. Jim informed me that the building alone had cost seven thousand dollars, and now it was a dreary, deserted place, turned over to the management of strangers.

I at once informed the Mexican in charge that he must quit the castle, for I had been appointed his successor. He immediately gathered together his belongings and vacated the premises, and I assumed the responsibility of managing the place. I had brought the pony with me, and when Jim and the Mexican were gone, as he was my sole companion, I took the faithful creature into the house, and put him in one of the empty rooms for the night. I had no bed, no chair, no table, nothing but some straw and a buffalo-robe. I found some wood, made a blazing fire, and sat down on the buffalo-robe. I could not expect any supplies until morning, and I decided to make the best of things. But meditation even by a pine fire did not prevent me from getting hungry; so, taking a torch, I began to forage for provisions. I was lucky enough to find the remains of the Mexican's supper, a bowl of "tobie," which at least filled me up. After eating, I lay down before the fire to rest if not to sleep.

Morning brought my friend Boyse with a team and wagon, boxes of bedding, of bacon, bread, and beans, and some cooking utensils. He was to be the farmer, and I the overseer and dairyman at the same time. Mr. Aley came from the Fort and brought me a peon or slave, who was to occupy one of the peon cottages, and whom I found a good old man, capable and willing, and fully acquainted with the details of a *ranchero's* duties.

Boyse soon grew tired of New Mexico, and demanded that Mr. Aley take him back to the States or to the Territory of Kansas. His request was granted, and in a few days, as Mr. Aley, the "Miadoma la grande," was gone also, I was the sole miadoma of the estate, and my only companions were the Mexican peon and his family. In sport, Mr. A. called me "John Bull," because I was an Englishman, and during my stay in the Territory everybody called me "Mr. Bull," "Señor John," or "Señor Juan." Mr. A. promised me when he left, that in June he would bring my wife and child; so I resigned myself to circumstances, and entered upon the duties of my position with as much patience and courage as the case would allow.

It would be impossible to enumerate the duties expected of me. Hotbeds on the inside of the spacious plaza must be prepared; a big garden made; the Mora river dammed so the land could be irrigated; a place selected for the trench from which the water was to be distributed; the fresh cows brought in from the Rio Grande, and the best ones selected for the dairy.

A good bed, chairs, tables, and a colored cook, had now been provided, and I was more comfortable. I had a mule furnished me, too, to use in overseeing the men. I bought two more peons, as now the crops had to be planted and the irrigating ditches prepared. Seed wheat was two and a half dollars per bushel, and I was ordered to put in ten acres of wheat. The only person having seed wheat to sell was an old Spaniard living five miles from me, on the Mora road. He was a great land-holder, having acquired large land grants from the United States at the close of the Mexican war, as concessions or rewards for his services in securing peace. This land he sold, not by the acre, but by the yard, or "varras." He kept thirty employés, and had twelve grandsons of whom he was very proud. Greatly prejudiced against "Americanos," he answered in reply to my request, "No tenny, no tenny, hombre (man)." One of his grandsons good-humoredly told me how to get the wheat.

"Send your peon—José Maria Barrella," he said.

I did so, and the old Spaniard, not knowing that he was my peon, sold him all the wheat I wanted.

I now employed two men to plow in the wheat. It was amusing to watch the plowing. Mexican plows were made of slender shafts of wood with turned-up handles; a piece of wood ironed at the point turned the soil; a big dry cow or an ox drew the implement, and a "moaria" or woman walked ahead as a guide, while the man walked behind holding the handles. There were no drills, and I sowed the wheat broadcast with my own hands.

The dam occupied the attention of all hands for some time. The amount of rocks, earth, turf and brush used in its construction was immense. This work done and the trenches ready, the water of the river was at my disposal. The land was laid off in squares, and the water turned upon it. Irrigators kept the water within proper bounds, and stirred the earth with hoes so the moisture would sink down and wet the soil. After a sufficient time had elapsed, ten acres of our experiment corn was planted by a man following a single-shovel plow. The crop made nothing but fodder, but ten acres of Mexican corn made a good crop. Thirty acres of Hungarian grass were sown, ten acres were made ready for the oats, two acres for California beardless barley, and three acres were left for sundries. Men with hoes kept down the weeds. The soil was a black alluvial, six feet in depth, and very fertile.

As yet the cows had not been brought to the ranch, and the men complained of the lack of milk and butter. I went to see Mr. A., who was just about to start for the States on his sutlership business, and told him how the colored cook was hampered in providing acceptable food through the absence of eggs, milk, and butter. He immediately bought ten cows and sent them to the ranch. I made all arrangements with him before he started for some necessaries for the ranch, and above everything else he was to bring my wife and child. I sent Lottie full instructions and advice concerning her trip, and urged the benefits she would derive from the salubrity of the climate. Mr. A. promised faithfully to carry my message, and upon his return to bring with him the precious charge intrusted to his care.

I now turned my attention to my work, and the days passed so rapidly that before I was aware of it the time for Mr. A.'s return was close at hand. I had put in all of the crops, and, with the assistance of my men, irrigated them. I had attended to my garden and hotbeds, and done my best to raise potatoes. I may as well say here, that I never grew them in New Mexico larger than marbles. The soil lacked something necessary for their growth. I also fitted up a dairy-room, and now awaited my wife's arrival before we began our butter-making.

I had on hand a large amount of materials for salads, and decided to take them to the store at the Fort and exchange them for articles for use on the ranch. I had a washtub full of pepper-grass, onions, lettuce, and other early garden stuff, and I drove a mule team to a wagon. The morning was clear and bright, with no sign of wind or storm, but before I was half-way to the Fort a fearful-looking black cloud obscured the firmament, and hailstones began to fall about me. I was four miles from shelter, and the mules plunged frightfully. The cloud made the air almost dark, and from it fell the most fearful torrents of rain, mixed with the largest hailstones I ever saw. With one hand I tried to hold the rearing team, and with the other caught the tub, turned out the green stuff, and put the inverted vessel over my head. I had to zigzag about on the prairie in order to save the mules, and by the time the storm ceased I had enjoyed the experience of Diogenes as long as I cared about it. My green stuff was all lost or spoiled, and my labor and my first prospective ten dollars were floating around on the prairie in a new kind of soup, to my own regret and that of the ladies in the Fort. But I was soon consoled for my losses by a letter from my wife, who wrote that I might expect herself and little Lizzie in a month, if they were not murdered on the way by Indians.

Flour was then very high in New Mexico; it cost me ten dollars per hundred pounds, and I had to send to Taos to get it. Labor was as cheap as provisions were dear. The Mexican who hauled the flour was gone four days, and charged me only two dollars. When I asked him how he could work so cheaply, he replied:

"It nothing cost on the way. Friends feed a Mexican for nothing."

The hospitality of the Mexicans was truly remarkable. They freely entertained friends or strangers, and disdained payment for their courtesy. Roman Catholics in religion, I found them a priest-ridden people, many of whom were so dominated by the worst elements in their society, that they were not to be trusted. But the great majority of the masses were kind-hearted, hospitable, and temperate. Drunkards were rare among them. There was hardly a respectable white resident near me. Half-breed Mexicans, Indians and negroes, many of whom were peons, and some of whom were thieves and worse characters, were the classes who sought employment, and therefore were the ones best known to me. The rich old Spaniards and native Mexicans were rare in this community, but there were some of them, and they were vastly superior in honor and intellect to the half-breed whites in that part of the Territory.

On June 20, 1859, my dear wife and daughter arrived. As I clasped them in my arms and recalled our weary separation, I resolved that only death should ever again keep us apart for any length of time; and I have kept my word. The growing crops, notwithstanding a delay in their growth caused by the bursting of the dam the day of the storm, encouraged me to think that prosperity would crown our efforts with success, and happiness seemed once more in store for us.

We were very comfortable now, compared with my past experience. Clean beds, good cooking, books, and many other unknown luxuries came with Charlotte and Lizzie. The dairy business was begun, and our plans were shaping themselves rapidly, when another terrible hailstorm visited us. The beautiful green wheat turned into a bed of straw; the grass crop was ruined. My wife looked over the dreary scene, and asked, mournfully,

"What are you going to do now?"

"Go to work *now*," I answered, as cheerfully as I could; "I am used to calamity."

She looked up at me as I sat on my mule, and burst out laughing. I had been over to the store and bought me some low shoes and a striped shirt. Her laugh was hardly complimentary, but I laughed too, and sprang off and kissed her.

"Time evens up all odds," I said gayly; "work will make good our losses."

During this last hailstorm two herders were badly hurt, two calves and half a dozen pigs were killed, besides the damage to crops. Most singular was the fact that, while hailstones fell by the wagon-load on my ranch, the storm extended only a distance of two miles. Mr. A.'s loss was heavy, but, as I was to receive one-half of all the profits, mine was irreparable.

The dairy business now was our last resource. We had forty cows giving milk. They were inferior stock and not very valuable as butter-makers or milk-yielders. I hired several extra hands, among whom was a cook, leaving my wife the care of the butter, and I the cheese. In a short time we made seventy pounds of cheese and thirty-five pounds of butter per week. The nutritious Mexican grass made the butter very excellent in quality, but the milk seemed deficient in caseine and did not produce as much cheese as it ought to have done.

In addition to my dairy work, there was much else to do. The wheat and grass land had to be replowed and put to some use. The products of my hotbeds—a thousand cabbage and five hundred cauliflower plants—were now ready to set out. The main herd must be brought from the Rio Grande, and (as it was not allowable to herd cattle near the Fort) they had to be kept at Ockata, about thirty miles from the ranch.

The negro, Jim Tillman, who first escorted me to Don Aleandro's ranch, was the chief herder. He was a dangerous man, who had been sent out from the States two or three years before for attempting to poison a whole family. I learned soon that he did not remain at his post very steadily, but would often leave the herd with the other men and go off for two or three days' absence. When there were fandangoes going on, he would kill the young calves and sell the meat. Sometimes, for gambling-money, he would sell a cow. I ordered him home to the ranch, but he did little better there than with the herd. He would steal my mule and ride him nearly to death of nights, and do other as disagreeable things.

One morning Jim was brought into the yard covered with blood. The two Mexicans who carried him said that he had run off and gone to a fandango, got drunk, and fought until he was nearly dead. I had to nurse him, and I became anxious to have him removed, as I feared my family were not safe so long as he remained.

Dr. Connelly, so well known as a Santa Fé trader, at last bought the negro, and promised to send him far to the south, and away from St. Louis. Mr. A. received two thousand dollars for him. The doctor was to start by the mail outfit, but was to take with him his own conveyance, and would use the slave to cook for the party. Mr. A.'s parting injunction to me was to bring Jim to the Fort, with his bedding and gun. So I flattered the negro, and took him with me to Fort Union. Dr. Connelly carried him off, and he troubled us no more.

I had been obliged to send my cow-herder at the ranch, Joan Garcia, to take Tillman's place with the main herd, and my peon, José Maria Barrella, took the herd. I was busy with my cheese-making, and could not watch him closely, and the first thing I knew the peon had run off to a neighboring hamlet, leaving the cows to graze at will. It took some time to get the herd of cows where they belonged, and by that time I was as warm as my mule. I went after the slave, and carried with me a small gun with a bayonet. I found him serenely enjoying himself with his old neighbors, and ordered him home. Seeing the bayonet, he fell on his knees, and turned his eyes toward heaven, presenting a most striking picture of contemptible humiliation. It was too much! I jerked off his blanket and kicked him — not for his offense, but because he could so far forget that he was a man, and then I turned away and left him. About two hours later, Barrella came to me, and touched his hat, and went back to his cows.

From that day until I left Mexico, he was the most careful man on the ranch. He stayed with me, and did such good work that I gave him his liberty, and paid him wages. All of the kindness bestowed upon him by myself and family never did him half the good that he received from my anger. His is the only instance with which I am familiar where a lift from the toe of a boot made a man out of a slave.

The other herders gave me almost as much trouble as Jim and José Maria. They would stone the calves to death, and sell the meat to their friends. If detected, they would say the little animals fell from the rocks and were killed. In spite of all reproof or punishment, they would lie and steal. They would allow the cattle to get away and go home, often at night, when they would destroy and overrun the crops. The six herders necessary to guard the cattle kept my temper constantly at boiling point. I had continually to scold, correct and discharge men — only to replace them with worse ones. Some of these kept women (not always wives) and children about them for employment in stealing. They lived in the peon houses, and they would steal milk by reaching through the corral and milking into tin cups. One fellow cut the canvas covering over some hogpens to get some stuff to make him a pair of pants. Another one stole my pony and hid it in some brush two miles away. It took me half a day to find it, and when I did, the man came with two others to meet the negro with me and myself, and fight us with stilettoes. We were armed with revolvers, and upon informing the thieves that the last one of them would turn his toes skyward if they interfered, they kindly gave me possession of my own pony.

One peon ran off, owing me twenty dollars. Some time afterwards, I went to Las Vegas to get some blacksmithing done, and upon entering the town I happened to see my missing peon. Like Barrella, he began to crawl in the dust of humility. I told him with more fervor than politeness that he was worthless, and need never return. The depth of my feelings or of my language must have affected him, for to my surprise, the next morning I found him at work.

Joan Garcia, Jim's successor, was a good workman when sober, but was drunk much of his time. His home was only a few miles distant, and his wife, a fine-looking Mexican woman, kept a small grocery and whisky shop. She asked me one day, when I had gone to look for Joan, how she could cure him of his terrible taste for liquor. It was useless to try to teach her the beauty of total abstinence, so I said, jokingly:

"Put a five-gallon keg of whisky near the door, and chain him to the door-post with a dog-chain. Put a tap in the keg and give him a tin cup. I daresay he will soon be cured of the habit."

I had no idea she would do it. But Joan was a little fellow and his wife a powerful woman, and she tried the suggested remedy. A few days later she came and begged me to go over and save her husband's life. I was a little alarmed at the turn my prescription had given the case, and at once went with her. He was dead drunk, chained to the door-post. She unfastened the chain, and I helped her to put him to bed.

"Diablos!" she said; "whisky no bueno [good]."

Garcia, during the two years I afterwards knew him, would not taste whisky. He came back to work, and was a faithful and honest workman. The Keeley cure would have been nowhere in his estimation beside a dog-chain and a full keg of whisky. His respect for me, too, seemed greatly increased. The harsher the method the better effect it seemed to have upon Mexicans.

Such were some of the Mexicans who served on Don Aleandro's ranch. There were Americans as bad or worse under my authority. I once sent one of the latter with produce to Fort Union. He was not back at milking-time, and I saddled my mule and went in pursuit of him. Failing to find him at the Fort, and uneasy about the cart and oxen, it being a lovely moonlight night I searched every nook and corner in and near the Fort for the man. At last, I found him asleep in a run, but it was a long time before he knew where he was, or the circumstances that had brought him there. As he sat up in the moonlight, he was a pitiful sight.

"Kill me!" he said. "I am of no account to anyone. I must have been drugged. I can remember nothing."

He roused up at last sufficiently to help me find the cattle, which were only a little way off. I coaxed him into the cart, and, when he had started, remounted my mule. In a few moments he stopped, and tumbled out of the cart on the prairie. Patience had ceased to be a virtue. I ordered him to get up. He began to fight, and we struggled together until he let me go and fell back, when I left him on the prairie in the moonlight, taking "solid comfort." He came in in the morning with two black eyes. When asked where he got them, he replied gloomily, "Mr. Bull knows."

During the years that have intervened since 1859, the changes in the customs and characteristics of New Mexico have been marked. More enterprising people have laid the Territory off in counties, and placed the foundation for a great State. The healthfulness of the country, the beauty of the scenery, and the advantages of soil and climate, cannot, in time, fail to make New Mexico a noted member of the sisterhood of States. The religious system which has placed such an incubus upon her progress is even now being lifted, and when that shall have been accomplished nothing will stand in the way of her advancement.

I found my little daughter a great help to my wife, and like a sunbeam in our household. She could talk in the Mexican language, scold the careless workmen while she milked nine or ten cows herself, churn and care for butter like a dairy maid, and ride her pony like a native. We had no schools, no churches, no society outside of our home for her, but she had plenty of pets and books, and was as happy as a bird in her new home. Dear child! in all the long years she has never changed to me. Her sunny sweetness to the adopted father who loved her as his own child has been constant throughout the changing seasons, and is as precious to him to-day as when on her little wild Mexican pony, a merry child of eleven years, beloved by all who knew her, she flitted over the prairies of New Mexico.

In the summer of 1859, Mr. A. became infatuated with Colorado. The excitement of the times concerning gold led him to invest heavily in the fascinating gold-digging business. Leaving me in charge of everything on the ranch, he returned to St. Louis, from whence he wrote me to send him at once all of the best cattle from the main herd, and two well-fitted wagon-masters. He invested in a machine for crushing the quartz, had it hauled overland from St. Louis, went with the train to Colorado, and lost thirty thousand dollars in the gold-diggings. Upon his return, his ranch was all the property that he had left. On the ground that few returned from the gold-fields, his stock became objects of booty to many persons who hoped he would never return. It was actually all I could do to prevent a Frenchman from driving Mr. A.'s entire herd off to California, and the rest of his property had to be as jealously watched and guarded.

The close of October wound up the dairy business. I sent out to the main herd by Barrella sixty-five cows and sixty-two calves, paid and discharged the unnecessary workmen, most of whom had worked all summer for six to eight dollars per month, and summed up results. We had made about eight hundred pounds of butter and five hundred of cheese during the four months just past. Our crops had not paid very well. The oats made only half a crop, but the ten acres of fodder sold readily at Fort Union for thirty dollars per ton. We had two hundred and fifty dollars' worth of Mexican corn for sale, and I had raised five bushels of beardless barley for brewing purposes.

In November it began raining, and such a ceaseless downpour I have seldom seen. I was not sure but that a modern Noah would be needed before the rain was over, to introduce a life-saving service for our rescue from the elements. Our adobe house, as was the custom there, was covered with dry dirt, and its roof was surrounded with spouts. These had been dry for so long that they leaked, and the constant rain played havoc with the adobe walls and dirt roof. The whole great building seemed in danger of dissolution. It took us some time to repair the damages, and prevent further ones from the same source.

I now prepared for the brewing business, which I had all summer kept in mind. With Barrella's assistance, I fitted up a fireplace in the fandango room, put a boiler of Russian iron over it to contain the boiling liquid, made a square chamber along half of the fireplace for roasting the malt, (part of which had to be a pale, and the rest a dark brown,) and succeeded in brewing excellent porter. At my request, my wife used it for her health until she was completely restored. I bottled some of the product, and the ladies at the Fort were greatly pleased with it.

Early in December, I sought the commissary and asked him what he would give me for my fine cabbages.

"Make them into kraut," he answered, "and I will give you a dollar a gallon for it."

I made a hundred gallons, and received a hundred dollars.

"You're a public benefactor, Mr. John Bull," said the commissary as he received it. "Who knows how many scorbutic humors you have prevented Uncle Sam's soldiers from suffering?"

I took him at the same time a hundred head of cauliflowers. The commissary presented them to the Governor at Santa Fé, and he sent me fifty cents a head for them. Of all my experience with this vegetable, the cauliflowers grown in New Mexico far surpassed the products of any other region.

Captain Morris, who had been stationed at Las Vegas, came to the Fort that winter, and he paid me a dollar per pound for the butter we had packed, some one hundred and fifty pounds.

Christmas Day came at last, and I looked around for some means of pleasing my wife and child. About midway to Las Vegas lived an American who owned a flour- and saw-mill and a dry-goods store. While dealing with him, he invited me to bring my family and visit himself and wife — a beautiful Spanish woman. I had an ambulance on the ranch, and, having accepted the invitation, my peon harnessed up the mules and we left home to take Christmas dinner with my new acquaintance. We arrived an hour before dinner, and were warmly welcomed by the gentleman and his charming lady. In deference to her, all of the courtesies of the occasion were Spanish. Excellent Espejo wine was offered us, and dinner was shortly served.

The dinner consisted of bread, baked in the conical

ovens of the time, *frijoles*, a kind of blue beans, and *chili colorado*. The latter was a popular dish among Mexicans, and consisted of a very hot, peppery mixture, made up of red peppers and chopped kid's flesh. As children were not then known as "kids," the compound did not frighten Lizzie, but my wife made her dinner on beans and bread. I enjoyed the *chili colorado* greatly. The meal was served picnic fashion — without chairs or table. Novelty made up for everything else that was lacking. We had expected roast beef and plum pudding, but really enjoyed our unexpected fare immensely, and upon our return we were loaded with rich presents by the lady, who seemed to have an unlimited supply of rare silk and satin dresses.

To our surprise, only a few weeks later, we learned that our host of Christmas Day was not a married man, and the beautiful lady was only the hostess for the time. Worse, he was connected with horse-thieves, and came near being hung by a mob of indignant Mexicans whose ponies he was trying to smuggle into the States. He had gone as far as Independence, where he was arrested and lodged in jail. But after eating pepper if not salt in his house, we could not help but wish him a better life.

Our next holiday expedition was to the town of Mora. The scenery of the drive was lovely. The Mora river, ever in view, wound in beautiful curves, the lofty mountains lifted their hoary heads into the blue sky, and the sunshine fell in white, clear light over all the scene. As we passed through the picturesque village of La Quaver and noted the piles of rocks and their accompanying crosses, it was like a glimpse of ancient Spain. Dozens of burros, laden until they staggered, passed us. We pitied them so, for when they fell they could not rise with their burdens without help. My wife remarked that we had either been carried back to the youth of time, or else we lived in the country of Balaam. "Surely," she cried, "the poor brutes are just ready to open their mouths and speak."

At Mora we found a quaint little Catholic church. We went in to the services. The beauty of the worship common to this religious people was either absent that day, or else my ability to enjoy it had not accompanied me. It was like expecting roast beef and receiving *chili colorado*. The waiting people did penance on their knees before their *padre* for a long time in silence. At length, still gazing upon their statuesque figures, he drank all the wine before him, and dismissed all but two culprits, whose sins, judging from the expiation, must have been enormous. These were taken out to the foot of the mountain, and provided with crosses heavy beyond their strength. The *padre* insisting, they started, barefooted and bearing the crosses, up the mountain. A whip was plied heavily upon their bare, bleeding backs, and blood oozed from scratches on their feet. The most of the crowd went back to their drinking and gambling, and we turned away from the scene. Saddened beyond measure, surprised at this unlovely pretense at religion, wondering if Jesus' death atoned not for these, we turned toward home.

The *padre* or priest in this service possessed a great fascination for me. Some time before that he had been superseded by another priest. The old *padre* was exceedingly jealous of his rival, and when the new priest on one occasion drank the wine as he blessed the congregation, he swallowed a lot of poison. As he fell to the earthen floor the people cried out,

"See how he is laden with our manifold sins!"

The old *padre* was tried for murder, and finally acquitted. After a short suspension he was reinstated; the people feared him more than ever, and he ruled them with a rod of iron. I knew him well. He often told me of his innocence and the thousands of dollars he said it required to prove the same.

In February I received word that a lot of relief horses were at the Fort, and that as the sutler, Don Aleandro, was gone, they would pay me seventy-five dollars per ton for feed. I immediately started out on a foraging expedition. There was no hay for sale within thirty miles, but by searching diligently I found around in nooks several jags of hay, which I bought. We camped without food near a timbered forest, as darkness and the heavy load prevented our reaching home that night. But in the morning, I reached the Fort with a ton, and received seventy-five dollars for it. The next day, with two yoke of oxen, we passed the scene where on the previous night we had guarded the cattle from the wild animals of the forest, gathered up a load of hay, and returned to the Fort. On the way home some cowardly rascals tried to stone us, but a discharge or two from a revolver sent them screaming away. The third load we bought at Ockata, and when it was delivered I received three hundred and twenty-five dollars in gold for my hay. I mention this to show the difficulty in obtaining supplies for the outlying military posts, and the high prices paid in order to obtain food for the soldiers and their horses.

The experience of the previous spring was repeated in the year 1860. Workmen had to be engaged for the irrigating, the dairy, and the main herd; seed wheat, at three and a third dollars per bushel, had to be bought; and the wheat sowed broadcast by myself, and plowed in with turning-plows. In addition, four acres of peas were planted to feed the large herd of hogs, and a fence was built to protect the crops from the carelessness of herders. Thirty acres of land were cultivated for corn.

In England the "corn laws" mean "wheat laws," but in America we call maize "corn," and the Mexicans had a kind of maize or corn which did well in its native soil. As different as the two names, were the methods used then and now of planting corn. Instead of the lister, throwing open a trench and depositing in it at regular distances the grains of corn, the seed was planted by hand in old-fashioned cross-rows, and covered with hoes. In addition to the crops mentioned, I planted eight acres of the California beardless barley, the yield of which brought me from the mail-drivers two hundred dollars. I tried no hotbeds that spring. The memory of my early products of the previous year being put on ice while I veiled my eyes with a tub, was sufficient for me; but I had a large number of cabbage and cauliflower plants, which promised good results.

The dairy business was as laborious as in the previous year; butter only brought, however, fifty cents per pound, at the Fort, but cheese always sold at high prices. That year we sold seven hundred pounds of butter and six hundred of cheese.

There was a demand for almost everything we could produce upon the ranch. Even the volunteer oats among the pea crop, when pulled up by the roots and hauled to the Fort for feed for some starving horses just brought from the States, netted thirty-five dollars.

The weeds grew so rapidly in this climate and soil, that

it required many extra men to do the necessary weeding, and make Don Aleandro's crops acceptable at the post. Some of these employés, like those of the last year, were not to be trusted. One of them attempted an assault upon me for removing his pony from the Hungarian-grass, and I had to drive the man off with a revolver. Fearing the alcalde's penalty of a flogging upon the bare back for his offense, he escaped, and we saw him no more.

I had employed an extra cook — Mrs. Brake, Lizzie and myself all being busy in the dairy; but with the great press of work, dinner was late one day. True to their custom, when a Mexican came along with a jug of whisky the hired men soothed their waiting appetites with firewater, and then whiled away the rest of the time with a free-for-all fight. The first I knew of the affair was later in the day, when I found kind-hearted Mrs. Brake binding up the broken heads. Indignant beyond measure at their carelessness of Don Aleandro's interests, I put on my belt and revolvers, and rode my mule down to the peon houses. Here I found a general jangle of wrangling voices, empty stomachs and broken heads. In my wrath, I drove the whole outfit out of the corral and down to the field. I had not eaten my own dinner, but I sat on my mule, revolver in hand until sundown, and made them work for life, after which they had to milk before supper.

After the weeding, I turned my attention to the swine, and found that my Mexican herder had sold three of them and used the money. He was tried before the alcalde, convicted of stealing, and punished by flogging. I was sorry for him, and resolved to keep closer count in the future. A superannuated priest then took charge of the stock, but the loss was as bad as before. He insisted that they strayed away while he prayed. I would not have blamed them if they had. He had to be dismissed. I inquired for him afterwards, and was told that he became so thin after the discovery of his stealing was made that he either vanished or the wolves ate him as they had lately done Lizzie's pony. I suggested that perhaps he had died, but the Mexicans shook their heads. An old physician who had just offered me his practice for forty dollars, said:

"They don't die in this healthy climate, unless they get killed. Otherwise, they just dry up and vanish."

The process of threshing wheat in those times was as queer as other customs of the Mexicans. After my ten acres of heavy wheat were cut with sickles, and shocked, I had an opportunity of seeing the grain threshed. Some Mexicans came with a gang of horses, and offered to do the work for ten dollars in gold, and I gave them the job. The wheat was placed in the center of a circle. The horses, eight or ten in number, were put in the ring, and two Mexicans drove them around with the heavy flails which shelled out the wheat. So cruelly would they beat the poor horses that sometimes the legs of the animals were broken. There were no winnowing-machines to clean the wheat. We made a sieve of rawhide, six or seven feet long, and filled it with round, smooth holes. Two stout Mexicans sifted the wheat through, and another sacked it up ready for the granary or the market. I lost twenty-five bushels of this expensive grain by trusting Pitts, an ex-commissary sergeant, to take it to the mill at Las Vegas. He got drunk and peddled it all out, and spent the money for whisky.

Hay harvest came with October, and a negro, Jim Waters, said he knew of an old grass-mower standing out in the open air some distance away.

"Take a span of mules, Jim, and bring it home," I said.

"There is a grindstone there, massa," he said; "we must have that too."

"How heavy is it, Jim?"

"About two hundred."

"Oh, no, Jim — not so large as that."

"By golly it is; and Boss, you must get a donkey to fetch it in."

"Why, Jim," I answered, "how can it be loaded on a burro, if it weighs two hundred pounds?"

"You jes' send Olean," answered Jim; "he know how to fix it on."

Olean was a powerful Mexican. I had seen him hold Don Aleandro's fine Kentucky bull by the horns until he twisted the animal down. I did not doubt his strength, but I was still skeptical.

"How in the Sam Hill can a man put a two-hundred-pound weight on a burro, and travel with it for thirty miles over a rough road?"

"Dunno Sam Hill," said Jim, showing his white teeth with a grin, "but Olean can do it."

"I'll give him an extra dollar if he does," I said.

Two days later, Olean and Jim appeared in the dairy-room. Olean demanded his dollar. The mowing-machine was accompanied by the donkey carrying the grindstone. The man would not unload, though, until I gave him the dollar, and I went out to see how he had managed the affair. I laughed as heartily as they did at the Mexican's ingenuity. He had stolen some stout canvas from my hogpens, made a sort of bag, and loaded one side with a kind of rick on which he rode, and the other with the grindstone. My ignorant mind was enlightened. I declared he had fairly won the dollar.

The grass, a rather light crop, was now hauled to the Fort and sold, and the pea crop harvested for fattening the hogs; the cauliflowers were again sold to Governor Rencher, at fifty cents a head, and the cabbage sold in kraut at a dollar a gallon. The peons were given their liberty, the cows sent to the main herd, and the work of the year rounded up.

In November, word reached the Fort that the Navajo Indians, many thousand strong, were on the war-path. The partially-civilized Utes hastened to the Fort for protection, and the white settlers at least were filled with the gloomiest apprehensions. Pickets were stationed around Fort Union, and the outside *rancheros* were cautioned to be constantly on the alert, to bar every entrance to their homes, and to forward to the Fort any information they might have of Indian movements. I was obliged to go over the lonesome road to the post very often, and one night was followed by a gang of Indians or disguised Mexicans. They were on foot, and were near me before I saw them; and as they began to throw stones at me, I fired four shots at them, and galloped homeward. My wife did not know of it, and in a few days the alarm died away without harm to anyone.

A few days later, news was brought to Colonel Crittenden, in command at the Fort, that some Indians had routed the settlers and burnt their homes, at a place where Raton now stands. The defenseless citizens were left to perish by starvation. Colonel Crittenden was so enraged that he ordered all hostile Indians that could be found — men, women, and children — massacred. Their horses, bridles, saddles, robes, etc., were to be brought as spoils to the Fort, and the soldiers taking them could retain them as perquisites.

I happened to be at the Fort when the soldiers arrived with their booty. A sergeant of my acquaintance said to me:

"See here, Brake — here is a fine mare. I shot a chief and took her for my own, as per order. This bridle and saddle were with her: ain't they fine? And look here."

He exhibited a wreath of twelve beaten silver dollars, set about three inches apart on a piece of silken material, and ornamented with beads of every color of the rainbow. At one side of the wreath was a woman's scalp with a tuft of lovely auburn hair nicely wrapped in red silk. It was a curious trophy, but strange to say sold, I was afterwards told, for a hundred-dollar bill.

I bought the mare, and Lizzie used to ride her. The animal had been trained to walk backward as well as forward, and would do so with my little daughter upon her back. I took the mare to Kansas with me later, but a Frenchman who worked for me during the war stole the valuable and beautiful creature.

Christmas Day found us still away from schools and churches, and with only comparative strangers to enjoy our hospitality. But my dear wife, remembering that it was our wedding anniversary, made one of her famous plum-puddings, baked us some bread and pies in the conical oven, and roasted a fine joint of beef, which she served with potatoes and cauliflowers. A bottle of home-made wine finished our repast. A kind-hearted German neighbor, Señor Weber, an old freighter across the plains, was present, and sang a German song. Christmas cheer was not lacking although we were far away from American civilization.

The thunder of Civil War was heard even in this far corner of the Republic, and its cloud was threatening to burst at any time upon our devoted country. I decided to return to the States as soon as possible, and began to make my preparations accordingly. The crops were sold, the cheese and butter put in the sutler's hands, my successor's comfort provided for, my resignation accepted by Mr. A., who had returned from Colorado, and a successor appointed, to whom I gave the inventory of the goods on hand. These were mostly articles retained for consumption on the ranch, consisting of pickled pork, salt hams and shoulders, kraut, buckwheat, Hungarian-grass seed, wheat, fat hogs, shoats, and several tons of ice — amounting in all to over three hundred dollars. Don Aleandro sent my successor with a friendly order requesting me upon leaving to put all of the ranch property in the hands of the bearer of the order. Very glad indeed was I of the release from the cares of my situation. It was yet a month until the first of March, when we were to start for the States, and we moved into a small adobe building until we could make our preparations for departure.

I intended to stop in Kansas for a short time, and then go on to Minnesota to take possession of my property. I accordingly gathered together for the expedition, an outfit consisting of an ambulance, the chief's mare, an old gray mare, and two ponies. After settling with the contractor at the Fort, I found due me on my sub-contract four hundred dollars. I did not like to carry it with me, and I intrusted it to Señor Weber, who freighted goods across the plains each year. He, fearing depredations from so-called "Jayhawkers," did not follow me for two years, and to the fact that I stayed in Kansas until I could receive this money, I may attribute my permanent settlement in that State.

The first of March, 1861, was a gala-day to us. We felt happy at the prospect of returning to civilization, even though we had to cross a part of the Great American Desert in order to reach it. A late snow-fall had melted, and the grass was springing up rapidly. The chief's mare and Lizzie's pony were packed, and all of our other supplies loaded in the ambulance. It was a fearfully windy day, and we only reached Fort Union. The night was a terrible one, and there was no sleep for us through its awful hours. I did not dare to leave the ambulance, and the horses could not be unloaded, for I could not even unfasten them for the force of the storm. My faithful dog watched with me all the night, and at last the light of dawn shone in the east, the wind fell somewhat, and with reviving courage we faced toward our far-off home in Minnesota.

CHAPTER X.

THE RETURN TRIP.

There is something invigorating in the thought of returning to long-absent friends, even though hosts of difficulties lie in the way; and, anxious to proceed, before we camped for breakfast that morning we were fifteen miles on our way toward the Raton mountains. Here we unloaded, and rested our much-fatigued horses, and then journeyed on to Ockata, where there was a good camping-place. I had decided to return by a different route than that taken by Don Aleandro in our trip to New Mexico. We would go through Colorado into Kansas, and strike the other trail at the Arkansas river.

At Ockata had occurred Indian troubles, but the Indians had been so severely punished by the troops that I felt little apprehension of danger, although I had with me the mare bought from the sergeant. It was a beautiful night, and the weary horses, as well as ourselves, enjoyed a good night's rest without disturbance.

We had our first wild meat at the Cedars, our next stopping-place, now a point in Colorado. With my flint-lock gun I shot a wild-goose which weighed, when dressed, ten pounds. Here we met an old man and his son who wanted to go to the States. The father decided to remain where he was, but gave us the boy — a stout Mexican — with his blessing. We found him quite an addition to our small company, and it was some time before we regretted having accepted the charge.

I had previously made an agreement to meet here a man named Inman, and his family, also on their way eastward. As he had two yoke of oxen and only one wagon, he had agreed to take a wagon for me, and some goods which I could not carry in the ambulance. We were to indicate our proximity by special marks, but I found none of these; and when I reached the Cedars, I learned that they had passed on without leaving any message.

I knew the marks left by my wagon-tires, and I tracked my treacherous acquaintance for many miles. From the direction taken I was satisfied that he meant to get to the Platte road, which diverged from the main road some miles ahead, and go to Pike's Peak. I learned from my new boy that two loaded wagons had passed about ten hours before my arrival. They had a lot of ponies and cattle, and seemed in a hurry.

To lose my trunk of valuables was out of the question, and I resolved to follow and overtake the fellow if it cost me a horse. So, very early the next morning, we started in his pursuit, traveled forty miles with only a two-hours halt at noon, and arrived at midnight at the Red river crossing. We could be only about twenty miles in the rear of the pursued. We were not so fortunate the next day, as I stopped to help a traveler's oxen out of a mudhole. But the grass along the river refreshed the horses, the delay rested my wife and daughter, and we were quite hopeful now of success. Ten miles farther on we came to a smouldering camp-fire. Beside it lay a pipe which I recognized as belonging to the escaping man. Confident now of being on the right track, and that our quarry was not far ahead, we drove off as merrily as did ever the racers after the Queen's stag in my old English experience.

In the passes of the Raton mountains, we heard the rattling of wagons ahead of us, and the chase became positively exciting. The stream had to be crossed and recrossed, and it constantly carried to us the echo of the wagons. It was as if nature sympathized with us, and, like a great whispering-gallery, held the echo of the guilty tread of the criminals fast until it was breathed into our ears. At last the sounds ceased, night fell, and we knew they had gone into camp.

In the morning, when the echoes again reverberated through the mountain passes, we resumed the trail. We were near enough now to hear the voices of the women, and the tones of Inman, who was swearing roundly at his oxen, but I did not wish them to see us until we were through the mountains: the diverging roads were a few miles beyond, and we could easily overtake them before they reached that point. Not wishing them yet to know that we were in pursuit, when we came to a ledge of rock over fifteen inches high that must be descended, I hesitated to make the necessary noise for the descent. There happened however to be timber near at hand, and a stout pole run through the hind wheels of the ambulance let it slide down the ledge with little noise and no damage. A little farther on we met the mail. Some of the men knew me, and yelled out as they passed:

"Going home, Brake? Company ahead!"

We now hurried forward, my wife anxious over a prospective scene, restless Lizzie amusing herself by counting the times we crossed the mountain stream.

"One hundred and twenty times!" she announced as we emerged from the mountains.

Five miles farther we reached the cross-roads. To my supreme disappointment, there was no one in sight. We had apparently lost the game. We camped in the triangle of the roads, and I waited for them to make a fire. At last, ahead of us a small smoke arose and mingled with the atmosphere over their camp. Then I sprang upon the Indian chief's mare and headed her toward Inman's camp. I was cool enough, for all my passion, but I was determined to have my property or know the reason. I looked to my revolvers and carried with me a bowie-knife. The noble animal I rode seemed to understand that I was on the war-path, and to exult in my rage. Swift and straight as an arrow the fleet-limbed creature carried me into the midst of the enemy's camp, where she paused, and stood like a statue while I vented my wrath upon the false friend who had decamped with my property.

I hope I may be pardoned for the classical language I flung at Inman. Remember, I had been away from churches for years, I was beyond the bounds of conventionalism, and even my wife and child were not within hearing.

"What in the name of Heaven, earth and hell," I shouted, "do you mean to do on the Platte road? If you don't turn your face away from Pike's Peak and come back to the road to the States, there will be blood in your accursed camp!"

Inman was surprised. He had not dreamed that I was near, and in his excitement he stammered out:

"We have lost our road; we did not know which to take."

"Then come into it at once," I said, "and prove yourself worthy of confidence."

Inman consulted with a fellow whom I recognized as a discharged herder of mine, and a lover of Inman's daughter. While they were talking I called the pretty girl to me, and persuaded her to go over to my camp and see my daughter. She consented, and in a few minutes the whole outfit had turned and driven back to the cross-roads.

They had been engaged in cutting up a freshly-butchered steer, and I learned from the herder that this steer was driven from New Mexico, and that they were not fleeing from me, but were afraid of pursuit on account of the animal, which until now they had not dared take time to kill. Be that as it may, I just missed losing my property. My wife was too nervous and worn out to be able to endure the rough scenes of a general camp. We made a fire to ourselves, and after thus seceding had the satisfaction of hearing our forced neighbors calling us "secessionists." We felt much better content alone. There were two families of them. A Mr. and Mrs. Bow had joined the Inmans in New Mexico. They had three cows, a pony, and a yoke of oxen; the others had two yoke of oxen, two steers, a pony, and my wagon. With my outfit we had quite a number of loose animals, which my Mexican boy now drove. He was relieved occasionally by the Inman children, of whom there were six, and he did not have to work very steadily; but, true to his native disposition, he began soon to weary in well-doing.

One moonlight night, my wife, ever watchful, screamed out my name. I awoke. Everything was still, but she told me that as she looked from the carriage at the bright night, she saw the Mexican sharpen his knife and start toward the vehicle under which I was sleeping. At the sound of her voice, he slunk back to his shelter and pretended to be asleep. We were satisfied now that he meant to kill us and take the team back to New Mexico. His actions grew daily more suspicious. Already traveling (although we formed a distinct and separate party) with a band of thieves, we were far from feeling secure. It was therefore with real pleasure that we learned, one morning, that our free gift was no longer our property. He had fled in the night — perhaps fearing that we might wish to detain him.

Meanwhile, we kept company with the Inmans — not from choice, but necessity. They had my property; I could not carry it. Inman, who was a sort of bully, pretended to "boss" the whole cavalcade, and, making a virtue of necessity, we kept our opinions to ourselves, along with our fire and our housekeeping.

One evening as we passed a whisky-shanty, the "boss" entered and filled up on corn-juice. He came out ready for emergencies. A few miles farther presented an opportunity.

"Halt!" he shouted.

We all stopped. Near by, grazing quietly in a grassy hollow, was a fine yoke of oxen. The "boss" shortly after drove them up to the wagons.

"How's that for a prize?" he called out, as he drew near.

Behind the wagon he drove he had tied some extra yokes. He did not stop to consult Mr. Bow or myself, but put one of these yokes on the oxen.

"These 'ere oxen is mine," he informed us. "They're a booty. Some wagon train has lost 'em."

THE RETURN TRIP.

Jane, his pretty daughter, chimed in with:

"Pa, when you sell 'em, I'm goin' ter hev a silk dress."

"'N me a suit of clothes," said the eldest boy.

Every member of the family laid claim to an apartment in the air-castle to be built by the proceeds of the sale of the "booty."

The "boss" unhitched his oxen, and put the new ones to the wagon. Then he came to me.

"Now, Brake," he said, in an expostulatory tone, "we've got a strong team. Take yer plugs out, and tie the tongue of yer carriage to the wagon. You can jes' set thar and be happy all the rest of the way."

"And be a party to a theft," I answered. "No, thank you; we are now very comfortable."

We traveled thirty miles that day before Inman would stop. At last we camped in a grassy hollow, and the cattle and horses were turned out to graze.

Here the women busied themselves with patching, washing, and baking. Such an amount of work those women seemed to have on hand! By our single fire, my wife and I agreed that the protracted delay of a day and a half was either to make us so tired we would go on without the "boss's" gang, or else to hide here until the owner of the oxen passed the camp. We decided to stay by our "stuff."

About two o'clock the next day, my wife called my attention to a man who had just come to the camp and asked Mrs. Inman for a loaf of bread. He said he was carrying a dispatch to Fort Wise; that he had a rifle to protect him from Indians, but was out of bread and had to buy a loaf. My wife, with her usual quick intuition, said:

"Depend upon it, he carries no dispatch. Look out for your Indian mare. I am sure there is some mischief brewing."

My wife's fears filled me with apprehensions. I knew the summary justice dealt out to law-breakers in those unsettled regions, and that we would in all probability be unable to prove our non-complicity in the affair of the oxen, if trouble arose. But we tried to make the best of the circumstances until we could get possession of our property, and lay down to rest as usual.

That night my faithful dog howled fearfully, and when we went out to see what was wrong, every hoof and horn belonging to our traveling companions had been driven off, except the two ponies. Not one of my animals was molested. The owner of the oxen had trailed them, hid his men in the mountains until night, bought a loaf of bread and fed them, and in the darkness, in retaliation for the theft, driven off the animals. While in the camp, he had satisfied himself that we had been no party to the crime, and had not disturbed our property. The advantage of our having kept a separate camp was now very apparent. They probably thought the two ponies were mine. I went up to Inman and asked him what he thought of the matter.

"Indians," he said, "Indians have run off with all of our stock."

"Indians would have taken mine as well," I answered. "Besides, I rode out and examined the ground, and found the tracks of American horses. The thieves are the rightful owners of the stolen oxen. You have brought this upon yourself. Now be a man. Ride after these men, overtake them, make reparation and secure your stock before they escape."

"I cannot, I cannot," was all he would say.

"Then your family, your friends, the whole company must suffer the consequences. There is no alternative."

Like a childish coward, the great bully broke down and cried. The despairing women and children wept, and the hungry baby, ignorant of the fate of the cow whose milk she drank, screamed in sympathy. The whole outfit seemed about to be dissolved in tears.

"Take us yourself," cried one. "Go after the cattle and bring them back," cried another.

"There are no Indians nearer than Fort Wise," I insisted. "The forces from Fort Union routed them, months ago. The thieves are white men, I tell you. You robbed them — face your own work."

"I cannot face them; they would kill me. You would be safe enough. Won't you go?"

I looked down at the sobbing group.

"Yes," I said, "for the sake of these poor women and children, I will go. Have your hired man, Robert, go with me. He can ride the black pony, and I will ride my daughter's mustang."

We started without breakfast. We expected soon to overtake the men with the cattle, and return in time for our morning meal. But hour after hour passed, and although we kept their track without difficulty, we saw nothing of them. Fifteen miles from the camp we overtook one of the oxen, and a little further another. They had grown lame and were left behind. Full thirty miles from our starting-point we overtook the men with the balance of the stock at a watering-place known as "Rocky Hollow."

This spot was close by a copse of timber, and the rocks hid numerous caverns and places of ambush; from these many a traveler had been dispatched, and justice seldom found a criminal who here took refuge. We rested awhile and examined our firearms. We had nothing to eat, so we chewed the cud of imagination and awaited developments. After a long time, Robert saw a man steal by a rock. He whispered to me:

"There is the white man who came yesterday to our camp. There is no doubt but that the cattle are here."

A moment later, he whispered again.

"There, he is passing the second time."

Robert was an ex-soldier, and reckless. In an instant he had brought his rifle to his shoulder and was about to discharge it at the man. Our lives would have paid the forfeit.

"Don't shoot," I said quickly.

"Why?" he asked, bringing down his gun.

"You are foolhardy," I said; "how do you know but that there are a number of the men? What good would it do to shoot one man?"

We waited some time longer, and at last saw the cattle being driven into the road by four armed men. Robert's bravery deserted him.

"We are done for," he said; "what could we do with four men?"

"I am not going back without the cattle," I answered. "Let us follow them."

I led the way, Robert slinking behind me as if he was the thief instead of the men he was advancing to meet. When we were within speaking distance, I laid my rifle down before me. Robert did the same, but he was trembling so that his hands shook. He said afterwards that it was a wonder the gun did not go off from careless handling and kill its owner. Two of the men turned the side of their horses to us and stood by them, with the muzzles of two very interesting guns toward us. I sang out to them as I approached:

"What is wrong? Give us an explanation. If an injury has been done you, we will give you satisfaction."

"Our yoke of oxen was stolen," said one of the men. "We wanted revenge, and pay for the trouble caused us."

"Neither of us had any hand in stealing the oxen, nor do the cattle you have with you belong to us. We are most sorry that you should have been robbed, but the man upon whom you are taking revenge is very poor. He has a large family, and a little baby is crying now because it is hungry and there is nothing for it to eat."

"He should n't have stolen the oxen," said the man.

"Granted," I answered; "but he claims that he took them up as strays. You did not say they were yours when you were at the camp. How do you know he meant to steal them?"

"Well," said one, "all we want is satisfaction."

"What will satisfy you?" I asked. "What will you take and release the stock?"

"Two cows," was the reply.

I replied that three cows were all the man had. Would they not accept one and let us drive the rest back to the camp?

They finally consented, and we got the stock together and started back to camp, leaving the men one cow and our blessing.

Darkness came down upon us before we had gone four

miles from Rocky Hollow, and we had to stay all night in a lonely patch of timber. It took us all the next day to gather up the lame oxen and make our way back to the camp. We were almost starved to death, and were hailed as deliverers by the anxious and despairing group awaiting our return. Only the man who had caused all the trouble seemed indifferent. The sufferings, the anxieties, the dangers endured, all melted together into insignificance beside the sheer ingratitude of the "boss."

"You must have druv them cattle purty hard," he remarked, as he removed his quid of long green and replaced it with a larger one. "They're e'enamost tuckered out."

We moved on as soon as the cattle were rested, toward Fort Wise. On our way we passed the dilapidated ruins of the Old Bent's Fort where, a few years before, the Indians had massacred about thirty-five persons — all of the garrison, and the settlers who had taken refuge in the fort. It was a melancholy sight, and called up gloomy reflections; but everything was quiet now, and we passed on to Fort Wise, reaching it the first of April. Here were a large number of Indians, survivors from Colonel Crittenden's severe chastisement. They had lost everything they had in the way of food, and most of their equipage. They had subsisted on mule-flesh awhile, and then swarmed around Fort Wise to beg help from the Government. One of them at once proffered me a mule for a trifling sum. Another wanted to trade me a pony for a saddle and a bottle of absinthe. But it was contrary to military orders to trade with them.

At Fort Wise we fell in with some freighters bound for St. Louis, with empty wagons, and a "cavillard" (Spanish for loose cattle and mules) driven behind the wagon.

That night, some of our company became acquainted with two of the privates in the Fort, and planned to help them desert from the service. Always ready to do a deed for the results of which he would be too cowardly to take the consequences, "Boss" Inman (as the men still called him) allowed these deserters during the night to pack their rations in the wagon I had loaned him.

I learned of it the next morning, and earnestly remonstrated against his allowing them to further accompany him.

"Pshaw!" he answered; "we'll be rid of 'em before we are fairly started. I mean to betray them. But my family are gettin' short on provisions, and I want the'r grub."

I did not think he would do such a thing. But I learned afterwards that he had intrigued with an officer of low rank for their capture. Sure enough! about four miles from the Fort, we saw the two privates camped in some brush. Suddenly two sergeants rode up to them. The privates, weary with their night's work and their rapid tramp, had fallen asleep, and they were arrested without trouble. The officers looked through our train and found the rations. I was afraid we would all be arrested for complicity in this serious matter, but true to his promise to Inman, one of the officers remarked with an oath:

"Let their rations stay there. These fellows won't need them. They'll feed on bread and water for the next six months."

Inman was a specimen of the class of people one frequently met in crossing the plains in the fifties. He did not evince the slightest compunction as the poor soldiers went back to suffer for their desertion.

It was a grand sight in the old "trail" days to see the "prairie schooners" with their white covers careering proudly over the desert. Sometimes a heavily-laden wagon would have as many as twenty yoke of oxen or as many span of mules attached, and often the string of wagons was a mile or more in length. Shouts of glee, merry songs, happy child-laughter, and the tones of women in conversation, made the long journeys a dream of picturesque and never-to-be-forgotten pleasure. Few that participated in those journeys remain to tell the story. Many of them long ago reached the end of life's trail, crossed the river, and are camping upon the plains of celestial light. Other scenes now are exhibited in the panorama of Nature than the hundreds of miles of lonely road, the occasional Indians, the wild birds and animals. The wilderness has been turned into a garden, occupied by civilized man. But so long as a single person who once crossed the plains over the Santa Fé trail remains, so long will pictures of that grand old time rise in his mind, and stand out in bold relief, unchallenged as to wildness and beauty by any other vivid scene of imagination or memory.

As we joined the caravan winding across the prairies, now comparatively safe from savages, and led by a lively and friendly wagon-master, our spirits rose, and we fancied that all dangers and annoyances were ended. Our late companions in travel had found conveyance in the freighters' empty wagons, we had regained most of our property, and now traveled in peace. Our progress was slow; some days we only made fifteen or twenty miles. The oxen were lame and weary, and some of them were sick from the alkaline water. We camped at night on the highest ground, as it gave us a better watch prospect, and we were freer from annoyance by wolves. One night in a valley below us, the howling of the wolves was fearful. Early the next morning the wagon train moved onward, and in the hurry of starting my gray mare was left alone. I sprang on Lizzie's pony and went back after the poor creature, but before I could reach her a large buffalo wolf had hamstrung the animal. I was not three rods from her when she fell backward, bleeding fearfully, and groaning with anguish. I had no time to lose. The train had moved on, and Lizzie and my wife were sitting in the carriage, nervously waiting for my return. I sprang off the pony, tore the blanket from the mare, flung myself again on the mustang and galloped back to my family. By the time I reached the carriage, fifty wolves or more were eating upon the still living mare.

Between Fort Wise and the crossing of the Arkansas river, we saw many buffalo carcasses. They had been slain, the hide and tallow removed, a few steaks extracted from the "hump," and the rest of the animal left for wolves. No wonder that the noble buffalo vanished from Kansas, nor that the antelope, disgusted at seeing wolves whetting their appetites upon buffalo-steak, disappeared about the same time.

Having crossed the Arkansas, we made our way to that earliest symbol of Western civilization, a whisky shanty, which in this instance happened to be still located on Cow creek. There were signs of human habitation to be noted as we neared the place. A man with a pair of buffaloes was breaking up a piece of raw land. We breakfasted on canned oysters, ham, eggs, bread and butter, and, as if to make the name of the place good, were offered milk from the cow and water from the creek. All this was delightful, but was counterbalanced by the vast amount of poor whisky dealt out to the freighters. It was astonishing how much money those fellows seemed to have to expend for liquor, and how much of the stuff they could put away. If ever men "put an enemy into their mouths to steal away their brains," it was the unfortunate men of the wagon trains. With less of the responsibility of an outgoing train to New Mexico, the returning freighters, always bent upon enjoyment, often sought excess at the first opportunity. The stuff called whisky, furnished at Cow creek, sometimes made the camps worse than scenes where escaped lunatics give vent to unbridled noise and passion. There seemed always in these long trains a commingling of various nationalities, and when all were fired with whisky, it was difficult to tell who were the worse men — Indians, Mexicans, Spaniards, or Americans.

The number of wagons camped on Cow creek was sufficient to form a large square, as a protection against marauders or intruders who might not be in sympathy with the fraternity of freighters. We had within the corral thus formed, over two hundred head of mixed stock — forty span of mules, and one hundred and fifty oxen. There were not so many men as usually went out to New Mexico with the freight, for it was customary to gather up a good many men that wanted to go to the Territory, and many of them did not return with the freighters to the States. There were several families, which, like my own, had joined the freighters for company, and each separate company had a separate fire. There were six fires outside of the square, that evening we spent in camp upon Cow creek, and when supper was over, the families were grouped about them listening to merry ditties and tales of adventure, all engaged in passing away the time. There was no light save from the burning embers.

I was watching the men who had been drinking at the shanty, and, as some of them began to grow mischievous, felt uneasy as to results. I took my carriage a little way off, and quietly closed my wife and daughter within it. There was a Canadian in the drunken crowd, who now began to go up to the fires (beside which still sat women and children) and stamp out the embers. I knew that when the fires were all extinguished, pandemonium would reign supreme, and I resolved to protect my fire. I had prepared myself with the heavy iron rod of my musket, and when the Canadian, having extinguished all of the fires but mine, staggered over to where I was sitting, I dealt him a blow across the head just as he sent his great boot at my fire. He fell with a heavy thud, face foremost, into the ashes. A man near me rushed at him, and as he did so the drunken gang close by raised an Indian war-whoop. Not caring who they fought, they seized the first person at hand. It happened to be the Canadian, who was just recovering from the effects of the blow dealt him. He fought like a tiger, but they dragged him down and threw him into the river, and when he emerged they forgot him, and fought each other indiscriminately in the darkness. No shots were fired, but clubs and butts of firearms were industriously wielded for more than half the night.

A sorrowful scene for persons entering the bounds of civilization presented itself the next morning. If we had stepped within the portals of the damned instead of the limits of the region inhabited by Americans, the scene could not have been more terrible. Black eyes, broken heads, bruised skins, crippled limbs, wretches on the bare earth and beds of straw, dozens of men unable to answer the call of the freighter, to yoke the oxen or harness the mules, were some of the features presented. Several half-sobered sinners were left without a dime to buy bread, and without pay for their previous work. It was a sad time to the poor fellows when the wagon train wound out of sight leaving them to digest their poor whisky and bad folly on empty stomachs and with unfilled purses. I never knew what became of them.

The extravagance of the men had caused the wagon-master to be out of supplies, and we were fifty miles from where he could purchase more. Although well stocked with wretched liquor, the trader at Cow creek had no flour to spare, and but for the surplus I happened to have with us, the men would have suffered from hunger. I let them have two sacks of flour and a hundred pounds of meat, and we resumed our journey.

At Cottonwood was a small dairy where milk and water could be had as freely as whisky could at Cow creek. It was amusing, however, how afraid freighters were of the possible effects of alkaline waters on the system, and the certainty that a flask of liquor was an indispensable aid for rattlesnake-bites. We saw the flasks much oftener than the snakes, though their owners had the appearance of being constantly bitten. We camped at Cottonwood, and spent a quiet night. The month of May with its healing breezes had come. As the tall cottonwood trees waved above us, the Kansas zephyrs seemed to whisper in our ears promises of sweet home life, and of peace and rest, not far off in the future, but near at hand. The murmurings of civil war, which had now increased into a burst of sound, were not distinguishable in this sylvan retreat. We were happy almost to gayety as we resumed the trail.

We soon passed Lost Springs, and camped in the Diamond valley. The next day, May 6th, 1861, brought us to the place of our destination — Council Grove, Kansas.

Inman got even with me for forcing him to turn away from the alluring vision of Pike's Peak. He had taken my wagon to pieces and loaded it with his supplies in the freighter's wagon. Then he saddled upon me the bill for bringing himself and family all the way from Fort Wise to Council Grove. I had to put the wagon together, and by this time it was as dearly bought a wagon as has ever been seen in Kansas. But victory is something.

CHAPTER XI.

LIFE ON A KANSAS FARM.

Council Grove, Kansas, in 1861, was a very different place from the same town in 1896. Only a few houses were on the site of the village, although it was growing, and throughout Morris county there was little in the way of improvements. The Kaw Indians owned the land on which the town was located, and so long as their title was in force it seemed useless to attempt permanent improvements. The beautiful orchards, the fruitful gardens and blooming flowers were then all missing from the landscape, and the bending trees and far-sweeping prairies on which the miracle of spring was just being wrought looked lonely enough. But we ate our dinners on the grass back of a Dr. Bradford's, (still an honored resident of Council Grove,) bought a quart of milk to drink, and rejoiced in being at last alone as a family, and within reach of cultured people.

We had no home, but a Reverend William Bradford loaned us a claim-house for one week, and we started for our new home — a log shanty in the midst of a sea of waving grass.

Indians usually select the best locations, and I decided that as I must stop somewhere until Señor Weber brought my four hundred dollars, it might as well be near Council Grove.

There were no newspapers to afford information at that time in Morris county, except a very amusing sheet known as the *Kansas Press*, published by Colonel Sam Wood*—well known in the early history of Kansas. And although the early files of this Kansas production were worthy of a place in a Kansas museum, there was little in them to help one in the choice of a location. Although Kansas was settling up rapidly, people came into Morris more slowly than into the adjacent counties, on account of the Indian titles to the land. Morris county had taken her part, however, in the early struggles. Colonel Wood and Honorable H. J. Espy had held seats in the famous Leavenworth Constitutional Convention of 1858, William McCullough in the Wyandotte Convention of 1859, and many of the citizens had ardently aided the Free-State cause. Now that the Rebellion had begun, her brave men stood ready to go at the call of duty in defense of their country, and their wives and daughters were as ready to bid them good-bye and God-speed as were the women of any other county in the State. Of the two men first mentioned, Colonel Wood afterwards served with distinction in a Kansas regiment, and Mr. Espy, then Colonel of the 68th Indiana regiment, laid down his life at Chickamauga to conserve the principles to which "Bleeding Kansas" owed her existence. Many other Morris county patriots deserve the mention which lack of space forbids.

A gentleman named William Owens, wishing to con-

---

*Colonel Samuel N. Wood possessed a remarkably forceful character, and in more than one case stamped his individuality on Kansas thought. Fearless to recklessness, by the rescue of a Free-State prisoner in 1855 he precipitated the Border war in Kansas, which resulted in making it forever impossible for slavery to gain a footing in the State. Standing by the position taken, he devoted his entire service to the Free-State cause. As a public officer he was a firm friend to education. With him originated the Kansas Normal Institute. Despite the faults which many claimed he possessed, Kansas lost a friend who had served her faithfully as citizen, soldier, officer, when he was cruelly murdered at Hugoton, Kansas, in June, 1891, by a man interested in a county-seat fight at that place.

tribute his support as a soldier to the Union cause, was attempting to sell his Morris county land so he could be free to enter the army. He had a half-section of land upon which he had "squatted," a one-roomed log house without a window, and a log foundation for another shanty. I bought both quarter-sections, and as it was not lawful to hold more than one, I gave the other to a neighboring squatter. We then moved into the house; the furniture consisted of one table, one bedstead, and a chair.

There were only eight acres ready for cultivation, and I at once had broken ten acres additional. The dry year of 1860 had discouraged the settlers so that they had made small attempt to turn over the sod; but plentiful rains had fallen, and there was fair promise of abundant crops. Grass was twelve inches high, and cattle were fattening rapidly.

The distress of the previous year was still severely felt, and aid from the East was being received by many Kansas settlers.

At the request of my neighbors, I took a yoke of oxen, and drove to Atchison, Kansas, where aid was being distributed to sufferers. Robert went with me. The materials had all been given out, and after buying for my own family as much food-stuff as my purse would permit, weary and tired from the long journey, we started for Morris county.

Returning, we passed through Topeka, then an extremely small and sparsely populated city, compared with the splendid appearance it presents at the present time. We camped near what is now the coal-producing city of Burlingame, and I was there caught in my first Kansas storm. It was typical of the hardships the State had endured, that many early settlers first met real calamity in a struggle for a livelihood within her borders. Wet to the skin, I took a severe cold, which settled in my eyes, and for a time made me nearly blind. Worse, it resulted in granulated eyelids, which has cost me much suffering and great expense, and was the first real personal affliction I had ever been called upon to endure.

On the way back from Atchison, we camped on a small hill near Auburn, Shawnee county — afterwards visited by Quantrell and his gang. There were several high brick buildings in the town, but the water was so vile that although the citizens dug deeply for purer streams, they had not then been found.

Tired and hungry, leaving Robert to attend to the oxen, I made a fire, and was busying myself about our meal, when a man, booted and spurred, rode up and began firing a volley of questions at me. He was evidently a politician.

"Did you come from Council Grove?" he asked.

"Yes," I replied.

"Did you ever hear of a man named Sam Wood?"

"Yes," I answered, looking up at him crossly — for his talk did not satisfy hunger.

"What do the people say of him?" was the next question.

"I am a stranger," I answered, "and do not take much interest in their talk."

"But what opinion did you form from their conversation?" he persisted.

I had a shrewd suspicion by this time of the identity of my interlocutor.

"From what I have heard," I answered, "I should suppose that he must be a d — d rascal."

"I am that man," he said, in a satisfied tone, and jumped on his horse and galloped off.

I learned when I reached Council Grove that Mr. Wood was a candidate for office. I hope the reply given him proved as helpful as he desired it should be in ascertaining the drift of popular opinion. He often laughed over our conversation afterwards, saying that was the hardest rub he ever received.

Upon reaching home, I tried to forget this wild-goose chase by plunging into the work of crop-planting. Life was far from pleasant in our new home. Squatters upon the Kaw lands, we were subject to abuse and afraid of being eventually deprived of our lands. Often our horses, cattle and pigs were stolen, and sometimes a pig would run home with an Indian arrow sticking through its body, apparently glad to have escaped even on those terms from the roasting-spits of its would-be captors. Under all circumstances, until the titles could be confirmed, we put up with privations and did with very little furniture.

During the summer of 1861, the fire of patriotism was burning at white heat. Kansas people almost as a unit insisted on the sacredness of the Union. Hearts flamed with a burning zeal to prevent a dissolution of the United States, and the ardor extended itself even to the Indians. The Cherokee Indians especially flocked to the service, leaving their vast herds of ponies and cattle at the mercy of thieves. In a short time the red patriots became great sufferers from this source. Two young men from Morris county, named Bledsoe, went into the Territory and assisted in the robberies. They were arrested by vigilantes, tied to a wagon, and driven off, while their captors riddled them with bullets. It was a hard fate for them, and a sad story for their mourning, desolate father; but in those times there was little palliation made for atrocious crimes. Men took their lives in their own hands, and at their own peril became marauders and guerrillas. If caught, they knew the result that would follow.

Great privations were endured by the settlers that summer, despite the prospects for a good crop. Flour was twelve to fifteen dollars per barrel, corn meal three dollars per hundred, bacon twenty-five cents and coffee sixty cents per pound. We used rye for coffee and a prairie herb for tea. All luxuries were out of the question. Those of us who from circumstances beyond our control could not fight for the country had no easy time to keep the wolf away from the door during those terrible days. If we never applied for a pension on the ground of the hardships endured, they were nevertheless severe.

In our own home we had secured a good cow, and with our prosperous garden were able to make a frugal living. Dried fruit was too expensive to be used, but we found some wild plums and chokeberries which took its place. I raised corn enough for my ponies and to fatten a pig for our meat. We had more cabbage than we could sell, and I made it into kraut. Altogether, we were not uncomfortable.

We had no mowing-machine, and as the time of grass harvest came on my neighbor put up the hay as fast as I cut it with a scythe. This work ended, we made the best preparations we could for the coming winter, and they were hardly completed when the second personal calamity of my life fell upon me. Hard labor and the malaria (of which the air was full) brought on a kind of fever and ague, accompanied by a chronic complaint which nearly cost me my life. The doctors gave me up to die, and when I recovered sufficiently to be able to work as I had previously done, a whole year had elapsed. The healthful breezes of Minnesota and the balmy seasons of New Mexico were very different from the climate of Kansas. The long-buried soil, now first turned over by the plow, filled the atmosphere with an effluvium so miasmatic in its influence that a man could hardly plow a day without an attack of ague.

The terrible sufferings endured for long, weary months, when for hours at a time I shook like a leaf, or burned like a red-hot coal, and the complication of diseases growing out of my prolonged misery, I shall never forget. I became as a skeleton, and lay for weeks in a semi-conscious state, only roused by the efforts of my faithful wife as she tried to force nourishment between my lips. Then a dropsy set in, and I was threatened with certain death. But at this time my brain became clearer. I had been troubled with all sorts of visions. Rays of sparkling and ever-changing light danced before my eyes, until the pain of vision became intense. A long ladder on which angels were ascending and descending was constantly in sight, and the most perplexing part of my fever was the placing by an unseen hand of a long row of ripe tomatoes. I was ordered to pick them one by one, and when the work was finished my sickness was to end. To my disordered mind they probably represented the years of my life. When at last I became conscious, I found myself raised in the bed in my dear wife's arms. As I look back to that day, I am filled with a happy gratitude that the Giver of life has seen fit to extend the term of those years to the present time, instead of permitting the angel of death to descend the ladder, and place my hand upon the last ripe fruit in the garden of my life.

I have mentioned my illness to show what the early pioneers of Kansas endured in their efforts to transform the prairies into farms. I cannot pass it without paying tribute to my heroic wife, who, like all other pioneer women of Kansas, bore privation, and suffered hardships to do her part in the work of settling the State we had both learned to love.

When I opened my eyes to a knowledge of my surroundings, it was a December morning, near the close of 1861; my wife told me that it was bitterly cold and was snowing. I was too weak to reason about the matter, but I looked at the fire burning on the hearth, and knew she was right. During the two months when my illness was at its worst, she and Lizzie, unable to leave me long enough to chop wood, had carried rails from a neighboring fence, put one end of a rail in the fireplace and the other out of the doorway, until it burned off, and thus contrived to keep warm. Both my wife and daughter had the ague by this time, and nutritious food was scarce in the house. Still, with the heroism that only a woman exhibits in such straits, Mrs. Brake nursed her utterly helpless husband and her sick child, and seldom complained.

At length, a preacher of the Christian church named Fisher found us, and came like an angel of mercy to our relief. He brought with him quinine for the ague, articles from which we could make nourishing food, and his team with which he hauled us a lot of wood. He also brought with him men to help cut up the wood, and never left us until we were as comfortable as sickness would allow us to be. If in recording reminiscences of Morris county, Kansas, I must mention a few people that were in those times weak and erring, here let me say that the deeds of this one minister of the gospel, if placed in the scale against the wickedness of all of them, would kick the beam to the ceiling, and cause to be forever registered in letters of light the superiority of the character of the great mass of the early settlers over the few who are so often quoted as representative of the early Kansas days.

But the sufferings of that awful winter have had no parallel in our family life. Besides the severe cold weather and the wasting sickness, we were the subjects of much loss. My Indian mare was stolen, my carriage seized for my doctor's bill, my other horse taken and sold by Indians, my saddle and bridle stolen, and my harness and overcoat loaned. As the winter passed away, we had little enough to eat. Lizzie and her mother shelled two sacks of corn and sent them to Council Grove to mill. Two weeks elapsed, and we suffered for food. Bran and beans were all we had to keep us alive. When the meal reached us we only received one small sack, but we were glad to get any of it back, and did not complain of the excessive toll.

The first relief of this time came to us in March. A Mr. William Polk purchased of us eight large walnut trees for a dollar apiece, and began making walnut shingles. With a one-horse machine they produced a fine quality of shingles — about the first of the kind made in Kansas. The eight dollars was a great help to us, and a little later, although far from strong, I went to work for Mr. Polk at one dollar per day as a sort of second sawyer in the shingle business.

After that the cloud lifted. One day when I was in Council Grove, I received word that a draft for four hundred dollars awaited my acceptance at Kansas City. My carriage was redeemed, my bills paid, and after hiring a man to break ten acres of land for me, I bought a cheap wagon and began hauling wood for a living for my family. When my debts were paid and a horse purchased, we had only a few dollars left. But I was recovering health and spirits, and while my loved ones at the house busied themselves in making butter and raising chickens, I managed to plant twenty acres with corn and potatoes. The prairie schooners still kept the plains dotted with their sails, and to the freighters I sold many dollars' worth of vegetables. Of cabbage alone, I sold seventy-five dollars' worth, and other stuff in proportion.

The war was now the topic uppermost in every mind. Each person by this time was placed in classification. He was either an "Abolitionist," a "Union Democrat," or a "Secessionist" or "Copperhead." People of opposite parties took delight in these names, and in calling their opponents by them. Kansas, as is well known, largely favored the Union cause, and from every county in the State men were pouring into the ranks of the Federal army. For myself, while heartily in sympathy with the Union, I was not considered either large enough or strong enough for a soldier. I was kept busy fighting the ague, which made frequent inroads upon my weakened system and overtaxed patience. My wife and daughter suffered, too, with malaria, and, being obliged to take much time to do little, the summer of 1862 was gone before we fairly realized the fact.

The prospects for a good crop were most cheering. But the task of putting up hay for winter was far from pleasant. There were no McCormick mowers, no sulky rakes with which to do the work. Only a scythe, fork, and rake, and the labor of a man shivering with a chill in August; but at last it was done, and a bountiful harvest provided for our stock, as well as a comfortable subsistence for ourselves.

The winter of 1862-3 was very cold. Snow fell in abundance, and ice froze a foot thick. It had to be cut daily to water the stock. Our shanty was in a rough part of the claim. Trees, gullies, snow-covered rocks, grew monotonous, and I began to try hunting with my flint-lock gun for a pastime. While strolling about near home one day, a flock of pheasants lit in the trees. Clearly, here was sport worthy of Nimrod. It would throw prairie-dog shooting into the shade. I banged away at the birds, and down two big ones fell. So did I! — and the worst of it was, I kept on falling. Down a steep bank, over and over in the snow I rolled. If it had not been for the decidedly chilly sensation, I would have thought the bottomless pit must be about to receive me. Never kicked a gun like that gun. It was some time before I recovered my wits enough to call for help. When Lizzie came to my rescue, the struggling birds must have greatly amused her, for she went off into peals of laughter.

Christmas Day was observed this year in our home. Pheasants took the place of roast beef and we had the usual plum-pudding. As we could not attend church, we read the Episcopal service from our prayer-books, and rejoiced in this day of days, commemorative of the event over which surely again "the morning stars sang together and all the sons of God shouted for joy."

The snow was deeply drifted in the hollows that winter, and through the month of January we were completely isolated from the world. No team could have reached us, but in February the snow began to melt, and a plan suggested to me by Honorable William Downing, Representative for our district, began to take shape in my mind. It was to the effect that we remove to Topeka, the lately made capital of Kansas, and educate our daughter in the College of the Sisters of Bethany. Being Episcopalians, it pleased us to think of sending Lizzie to a school of that denomination.

I was still a "squatter" upon the Kaw lands. The Indians held the titles to a twenty-mile-square tract of land on which Council Grove was located, and land-sharks, Indian agents, the Indians, and the settlers were mixed up in ceaseless contentions concerning the action of the United States Government as related to these lands. So I decided to take Mr. Downing's advice. I went to Topeka and secured a house and twelve acres of land, about a mile northwest of the business part of the town and south of the Kaw river. The house was one of the best then standing in Topeka, and was built of brick and stone. The grounds were a small nursery and garden.

Upon my return from Topeka, I learned that word had been received from Washington that the settlers might bid on the lands. An influential person at Washington, named Blacklidge, had agreed to accept five dollars from each settler and secure to all their claims, providing the bids were all right and in accordance with the appraisement. I at once sent him the five dollars and my bid, and awaited developments. I then rented my claim by contract to two men, named Sharp and Armstrong, after which we packed up and started for our new home.

Our road to Topeka was over the old Santa Fé trail. There was no railroad, and we went overland with a team, a pony, two cows, and a calf. We made half the journey in one day, and camped at night with the heavens for a canopy and the twinkling stars for companions. We were very tired, and congratulated ourselves on being so near our new home. A hired team had gone forward with our goods and a young calf, whose mother we drove with the other cow.

In the morning, to our dismay we found that horses and cattle had decamped. Only a pony remained to tell the tale that we had started with live stock. After searching for two hours, I at last concluded that the animals, not caring to be city creatures, had eschewed the bovine fashions of Topeka and gone back to the primitive enjoyment of their Kaw companions. There we were, like stranded pleasure-seekers with no sail in sight. At last an empty wagon came along and took us on to Topeka. A pitiful bawl from the motherless calf which had preceded us greeted us by way of welcome. As soon as I could leave my family, I went back after my missing stock, but although I sought them almost with tears, they were inflexible and kept out of my sight. They had not returned to Morris county. The prairies, the hills, were scoured without results. I finally reached a German settlement on Mill creek. The settlers, a thrifty people, could not speak English, and were so timid that they were afraid of my military overcoat which I wore to protect me from the cold March wind. They entertained me free of charge, but could give no information concerning my property. For a week, I searched among those high hills and deep valleys without success. At length I met a German who could speak English, and he told me where the horses were grazing. After some further delay I found the cows. One of them had not been used to a woman about her, and had kicked the good German lady who did the milking. A dislocated shoulder was the result, and before I could get "Madcap" I had to pay the lady's doctor bill.

CHAPTER XII.

A STAY IN EARLY TOPEKA.

There were less than eight hundred people in Topeka when I settled there as a resident. Only a village as yet, but with mighty prospects before it. The more than thirty thousand people, the splendid churches, institutions, buildings, well-paved and lighted streets, the trolley-cars, of to-day, only existed, if at all, in the mind of some visionary dreamer. The wonders of electricity were then unknown — the electric light and motor were locked in the brain of the "Wizard." But even then Topeka had that first accessory to the real Kansas town, an excellent college, and the pastor of the Episcopal church, the Reverend Mr. Preston, superintended its work.

I took my twelve-year-old daughter to the school, and she became a pupil. We united with the Episcopal church, and remained in this connection during our stay in Topeka. Reverend Peter McVicar was then the Congregational minister in that little city, and I greatly valued his friendship.

April, 1863, found me very busy as a market gardener, raising all of the products usually grown for immediate sale, and devoting much time to the nursery business. Those were the dark days of the war, when many women were left helpless and alone to support themselves while their husbands fought for their country. It was a pleasure to devote every odd moment to the succor of the widow and fatherless, and many pleasant hours were passed by myself and wife in assisting the families of dead soldiers during this terrible time, and encouraging those whose husbands and fathers still lived to hope for their safe return.

August 21st, 1863, occurred the terrible guerrilla raid upon Lawrence, Kansas. The notorious leader Quantrell led his villainous band into the place, in cold blood shot down the majority of the male citizens, burned the principal part of the town, and left the wailing women and children to mourn their cruel and untimely losses.

This alarming and shocking catastrophe, falling upon a sister city, threw Topeka into a state of consternation. The suspense and apprehension weighed heavily upon every person, for Topeka, like Lawrence, was loyal to the Union cause, and in its almost defenseless condition could expect no better treatment than had been received by that city. Our horror of an attack was increased by a visit to the ruins of the stricken town of Lawrence. The sight of the once pretty and thriving little city, now in ashes, was the saddest spectacle we had ever witnessed.

A few days after the Lawrence Massacre, a report reached Topeka that Quantrell was about to march upon that city. It would be impossible to describe the scenes that followed. Men, women and children ran hurrying about, shouting, screaming, moaning, as if crazed. Horses, mules, cattle and dogs were loose; saddles, bridles, harness and yokes were scattered about indiscriminately; a man with a thousand head of sheep was driving them into the Kaw valley to prevent their being driven off by the marauders, and everything was hurry, excitement, and confusion. A line of pickets was thrown around the city, and every person passing was challenged by the guards. My house, being a good-looking one, would probably be raided, and Lizzie and my wife were busily engaged in removing from its doomed walls everything too cumbersome or heavy for Quantrell or his men to care about disturbing. Perhaps they intended after awhile to remove the more valuable things. If so, in common with all the women of Topeka, they expected the guerrilla leader to grant them unlimited time to complete their arrangements.

The mail-carrier from Council Grove came along presently, and asked me if we should go into the timber and hide.

"No," I answered, "let us go down town and face the foe. You take my pistol, and I will carry my Harper's Ferry musket. We will get ammunition at the store."

So down town we went. The pickets stopped us; then, recognizing me, said:

"Go on and do your best."

Two ladies interposed.

"Oh," cried one of them, "suppose they are rebels!"

"No they be n't," was the picket's rejoinder.

So we went on into the main part of the town. Such confusion I never saw! Everybody was talking, and the men were busy loading their firearms, buying ammunition, and all were intent on greeting the guerrillas with a warm welcome. At two o'clock in the morning I said to the mail-carrier:

"It is all a hoax. Go to your hotel. I am going home."

Everything was out of the house, and it took most of the remainder of the night to get beds and bedding enough extricated from the general debris to furnish sleeping-places until morning. The ingenuity of those women in finding hiding-places for their treasures was wonderful. The morning presented a sorry scene. My fences were broken down, my growing crops destroyed, and our home ransacked as badly as if the guerrillas had gone through it, leaving only the walls. But we had kept busy, and that was very satisfactory.

Our minister, Mr. Preston, was visiting in New England. Mrs. Preston was in great anxiety about the plate of the church, and also of their own home. She sent me word about it, and I took a vehicle and carried the silver to a log house in the country, where I left it with a Mr. Covel, until Mr. Preston's return.

I was fortunate enough to dispose of my damaged garden-stuff to the landlord of the principal hotel in Topeka, and in September was free to give my attention to other matters.

I received word about this time that my bid on my claim had been granted. Feeling that my interest should center upon my farm, I began, now that I knew it to be my own, to prepare to return to it. We had made many warm friends by this time in Topeka, and these, with the seminary advantages for my daughter, formed ties that bound us to the place. But as we must depend upon my labor for support, I concluded we would be more comfortable upon the farm, and so it was settled.

I had promised certain persons to put up hay for them before I left the city, and as some of the parties were women whose husbands were in the war, and they had only the meager thirteen dollars per month to live upon, I promised to take whatever stock they could easily spare as pay for my arduous labor. I had to go five or six miles to find grass, and then it was slough-grass. I had no way to cut the hay except with a scythe, and no help but a boy. But the contracts were all filled, my goods packed, and myself and family on our way to our farm in Morris county by October 8th, 1863.

CHAPTER XIII.

BACK TO THE FARM.

What was most singular for that time of year, it snowed all day; and for twenty miles on our journey there was not a house for shelter. Five miles further, however, were the mail-house and stables, and here we put up for the night.

We found our home the next evening in a very forsaken and dilapidated condition. One of my renters had gone to the war; the other, lazy, disgruntled, or idiotic, had raised nothing, and finally deserted the place. It had only been through the kindness of a friend that my right to the place had been secured, for, although my bid was the highest, another individual came near getting it. As I looked sorrowfully at the forest of sunflowers, some of which were twelve feet high and had to be cut with an axe, and at the dense growth of poisonous weeds that covered every fertile spot, I felt how difficult it was to make a home in Kansas.

I had brought with me sixteen head of stock, but slough-grass was abundant, and the settlers had plenty of corn and oats to sell; so we were soon prepared to winter our stock. When the log cabin was repaired, we were ready for the winter.

I was elected justice of the peace that fall, and served in that capacity for the term. It was not a very lucrative business, for there were so few settlers in the township we could not afford law-suits. I always tried to fill the office of peacemaker rather than of justice, and it is very satisfactory to me that during the entire time of my incumbency not more than half a dozen cases came to trial.

Council Grove, being on the line followed by the freighters, had become a thriving place. There were still numbers of mules, horses and oxen kept there for service in crossing the plains, and the place afforded a ready market for all sorts of produce. Owing to the war, groceries were still very high, and besides this drawback, our stock was in constant danger from both white and Indian thieves. But I held on — watched, worked, and stayed with Kansas. A school opened about two miles from us, at the place where Kelso City now stands, and during the school season Lizzie would saddle her pony, ride to school, and return in the evening as she went. Sometimes, frightened at approaching Indians or suspicious-looking whites, she would ride for her life. Children did not find it easy to acquire an education in the early Kansas days.

In January, 1864, having run out of money, I turned my attention to the resources of my claim. I had about forty acres of fine timber, and I took a contract to furnish the saw-mill at Council Grove with a lot of cord-wood and posts. This occupied the winter, and the month of March was taken up in hauling the forest products over the eight miles to the Grove. In February, I paid for my claim in Kaw land scrip, and at last felt that once more we had a home of our own.

I sowed ten acres of wheat on the 10th of April, and it snowed bitterly all the time I was sowing and my hired man covering it with a turning-plow. When the wheat was harrowed in, I broke my land for corn, the seed for which cost two dollars per bushel. Those times furnished no improved methods of farming. We plowed deep and planted the corn as we did in New Mexico. But by proper cultivation, I often raised from sixty to seventy-five bushels of corn per acre.

During the closing months of the war, the Kaw Indians took great liberties with the property of settlers. The agency was only six miles from my place, and on pay-day the agents often paid them in dry-goods, plates, and trinkets. The Indians would go around among the settlers and sell these things, and when they saw an opportunity always improved it by carrying off a fat pig or a puppy. They were extremely fond of fat roasted puppies, and a little one I had would hide so long as the faces of the Indians were toward the house. As soon as their backs were turned, she would fly after them, bite their heels and bark, and the Indians would look over their shoulders eager to seize her if no one was watching. Pigs and heifers were often missing. The lazy Kaws despised work, and seemed to think the settlers on their lands owed them a living.

There was many a saddened home by this time in Kansas. Brave men had gone to the defense of the Union and never more returned. The gloom had settled like a pall over State and Nation, and our own little county was no exception to its universality. For miles around us it seemed as if all of the able-bodied men had gone to the war. Delicate women did the work of strong men, and lived on, hoping for better days. In one family there were only two girls to maintain their invalid father and mother, but they bravely took the place of their three brothers, and plowed and farmed forty acres of land.

The heat was intense that spring and summer. Sometimes, as I took my way southward with the wood I continued to haul to Council Grove, the air felt like the breath of a furnace. The man who laid down in the burning lime-kiln to die because the "unpardonable sin" was found within his own breast, might have saved time by stopping in Kansas during a hot season, and stretching himself upon a sun-exposed prairie. He could reasonably have expected that a chance comer would have found as white a skeleton as the villagers found in the kiln.

I had no reason to complain of the results of that year's work. My wheat made two hundred bushels, and was worth a dollar a bushel. All of my crops, including the fine potatoes raised on my new land, found a ready market in Council Grove.

December set in with a terrible snow-storm, and I prepared to fulfill a contract I had made to winter a lot of Texas cattle. There was a craze among the farmers of Kansas that year over this stock. Many invested largely in the cattle because they could be bought so cheaply, and many others, like myself, took them to winter on the shares. But these long-horned animals were too loyal to the Lone-Star State to become "jayhawkers." They pined for the mild climate of Texas until the cold winds of Kansas nearly blew through their thin bodies, and then they lay meekly down to die. The worst of it was, it took them so long to accomplish their decease. One old steer got down, and after I had carried him hundreds of buckets of water and fed him fifteen bushels of high-priced corn, he bade farewell to Kansas without ever taking the trouble to get up out of his tracks. Of the forty in my contract, I saved ten, and received five of them and a good cursing for my pay. But the experience was worth the trouble. I have never since undertaken to drive Texas cattle out of their temples of yucca and cactus.

The closing scenes of the war, when the soldiers laid down their arms and returned to the pursuits of peace, the death of the idolized Lincoln, and the stormy times that followed with the reconstruction of the Confederate States, absorbed every mind during the spring of 1865. But I raised good crops that year, and was becoming well pleased with my farm, when the soldier brothers of the girls who during the war had farmed the claim next to mine came home. Dissatisfied with the idea of farming, they persuaded Mr. Bowser, their father, to sell his farm to me.

Before we left our first home in Kansas, which we sold upon buying the other, a terrible freshet occurred. The creeks and rivers overflowed, and the thundering of the waters, the swirl of mighty logs in the rapid currents, for two days and nights, were awful. The water of Slough creek came up around my cabin, and washed the soil away from my corn. It was the first experience of the kind we had suffered, and, as we were not sure that our ark of refuge could stand the storm, it was with real relief we at last watched the waters subside.

Although I was given possession of our new estate and the patent was signed by Abraham Lincoln, I did not secure a warranty deed until September 17, 1867. The new house was a good two-story log building having a large fireplace which connected with a capacious rock chimney. In it, we were hardly pioneers any longer.

I tried diversified farming in the spring of 1867. Ten acres each of corn, spring wheat, and oats, five of millet, some potatoes, buckwheat, and a number of smaller crops were planted, as Kansas soil and climate were too uncertain to depend upon one kind of product. The season was dry, and crops were considered a failure. But I had learned the value of irrigation in New Mexico, and there was plenty of water in Munkers creek; so, by some effort, I saved all of my garden. A pest of almost invisible insects had invaded my cabbage-patch. I raised the plants in large boxes elevated four feet above the level of the ground; then I watered them morning and evening both before and after transplanting them, and sold from this vegetable alone over seventy-five dollars' worth of produce.

About this time, the Missouri, Kansas & Texas Railroad was built through Morris county; and as Judge Huffaker, the former Kaw Indian teacher, had a contract for furnishing part of the ties for this road, the settlers had a reasonable hope of making some money even though crops had failed. Morris county had waited a long time for a railroad, and the prospects now opened up were most alluring to the settlers.

Bonds were voted, and Judge Huffaker, who was to furnish the ties from Parkerville to Council Grove, opened a large store for the accommodation of the workmen.

Our native timber furnished the ties. I was to provide two hundred oak and walnut ones at seventy-five cents apiece. I employed four men at a dollar, and an overseer at a dollar and a quarter per day, and my ties were made, delivered and paid for before spring. A Mr. Parker and a Mr. McKensie were pushing the grading of the road, and it was carried forward with so much energy that by the spring of 1868, Council Grove had a good depot, and was a town on the new railroad. The rejoicing of the people was general, and many were the extravagant prophecies concerning the future prosperity of the town. But when Council Grove changed its place as the great rendezvous of freighters over the Santa Fé trail for a station on the road to Junction City, she bartered away much of her success as a town. However, it was pleasant to know that at last we were in touch with the State, the Nation, and the world at large.

It was wonderful, the amount of fruit grown in Kansas by 1867. Apples, peaches, plums, strawberries and grapes were abundant, and gave rich promise of the greater fruitfulness yet in store for horticulture in this State. True enough to this promise, two years later, at Philadelphia, the gold medal of the National Pomological Society was awarded to Kansas. As early as 1863, when I left Topeka, there were bushels of peaches rotting upon the ground. I selected a bushel of choice seeds and planted them in rows twelve inches apart. They grew rapidly into thrifty little trees, and I set out as many as we wanted and gave a thousand away to early settlers in the county. In four years' time, the yield of peaches was so prolific that all near us had as much of the luscious fruit as they wanted. Apples pay better than peaches now, but on the new lands of those times every kind of fruit seemed to flourish. It is well known that Kansas has sustained the reputation of 1869 as a fruit-producing State. In 1872, she received a diploma from the American Institute for one hundred and ninety varieties of apples; and in 1876, the diploma of the Centennial Commission for the best ninety-six varieties of apples there exhibited. Since then, even Queen Victoria has ordered apples from Kansas — "Jonathans" at that. The world has heard of Kansas fruits, and her fame as a fruit-growing State is not yet at its height.

On April 24, 1867, an earthquake shock was felt in

Kansas. It was accompanied by a deadly roar that sounded like thunder. I had an Irishman named Mike Miller working for me, and I called out to him:

"Mike, what is that?"

Only the whites of his eyes were visible, and he was shaking worse than the exigencies of the case demanded. He replied:

"The — the earth is shaking."

Sure enough! the ground was shaking violently, and when we went to the house Lizzie and Mrs. Brake were terror-stricken. Plates, cups and saucers had danced about upon the table, and the house had seemed as if rocking. This experience is worthy of mention for its uniqueness, and none of us have since had a curiosity to witness the shaking of the earth during a shock.

Chinch-bugs visited Kansas in the years 1869 and 1870. They fattened on my millet like pigs in a corn-bin, and, while they did not disturb the wheat very much, otherwise they did great damage. Potatoes were a poor crop in 1870, and corn was worm-eaten and the ears small. Tea wheat only made half a crop, and if it had not been for my beautiful white wheat, which brought me two dollars a bushel and afforded a splendid yield, we would have done badly as farmers that year.

I decided, as a sort of recompense for my crop failures, to invest in something that would lead to better results in the future. So, scorning Texas cattle as a paying investment, I bought a lot of sheep. I had it all figured out. Good fine wool brought forty cents per pound; as sheep cost about two dollars per head, the clip from a good, full-grown animal would nearly pay for its cost. The early part of the winter was so mild that on Christmas Day we ate our roast beef and plum-pudding without a fire in the fireplace. But it was cold later, and I built a circular pen for the sheep, with an entrance into and out of it. It was a pleasure to watch them on cold days pushing their way into their warm quarters and there hiding from the weather. I really enjoyed the care of them, but notwithstanding the "sheepish" enjoyment I took in wintering them, they did not pay much better than did the Texas cattle.

About this time I received a letter from my old home in Excelsior, Minnesota. As it embodied the general characteristics of life in Minnesota, I in part reproduce it:

"EXCELSIOR, MINNESOTA, February 7, 1870.

"MR. H. BRAKE—*Dear Friend:* I was about as much surprised to receive from our postmaster a line by your hand as if I had heard that you had risen from the dead. For years it has been reported and fully believed that you and your family were massacred by Indians soon after leaving this place. I am glad to learn that such was not the case.

"You see that I am still here. Excelsior does not prove to be among the rapidly-growing places of our State. The population is about the same as when you left. There are a few more dwelling-houses, and of a better class than the old ones. Some of the old ones are repaired, and the poorest are tenantless. A better church has been built.

"Your old farm is unoccupied; it has been in several hands. A Mr. Booth, living in New York, owns it now.

"The Gideons, Latterners, Days, Babcocks, and McGraths are still here. The principal business of the town is keeping boarders, as Excelsior is much patronized as a watering-place. Your old friend, Dr. Snell, with his family lives in Minneapolis. Morse, the blacksmith, is still here. Charles Galpin is in the dentistry business.

"My salary has always been small. I have succeeded in supporting my family by engaging in farming. Have used vacant lots and reclaimed much land near the lake-shore. My health is poor, and on account of my throat I have sometimes to desist from preaching. I still have 'Charley,' the horse I bought from you in 1858. He is getting old, but does well, though he now only eats ground feed.

"You left some deeds in my care. I cared for the lots for years, and finally bought them at a tax sale. There is no redemption law in Minnesota. I had your property recorded in your name, and paid the expenses upon it for you until I believed the story of your death. I have several lots that cost me ten dollars apiece. As I am not willing to hold your property since I have learned that you are living, I now make you an offer of twelve dollars each for the deeds in fee simple. Please let me hear from you at once.

"The college scheme of Mr. Galpin was abandoned, and the lots reverted to their original owners.

"Write soon about yourself and family.

"With best regards to you and yours,
CHARLES B. SHELDON."

As soon as possible, I accepted Mr. Sheldon's offer and gave him a warranty deed for the property. Mr. Sheldon sent me the money, and we corresponded with each other for many years afterward with pleasure. His letters were like glimpses, to me, of the lovely moonlit lake, the grand, wind-swept forests, and like the breath of the invigorating breezes of Minnesota. They brought vividly before me the little church, the kind friends, and helped me to be a better man, living not only for this world, but to meet those friends in the life beyond.

A great calamity fell upon us during the summer of 1871. My daughter, while climbing into a wagon, twisted her right limb and slipped her knee-cap. It was some time before her quick steps flitted through the house and over the farm as usual, and fretting made her anxious and unhappy. A physician came and put the bone in place, but, a terrible storm coming up, he had to remain over night with us. When his bill came, it included the item of detention, and reckoned up to twelve dollars and thirty cents for one visit. It was the only time I ever was charged for entertaining a man, and I insisted to Mrs. Brake that the character of her famous cooking was at stake, and that her hospitality must have been fearful in the extreme.

My daughter, about the time she recovered, learned of some newly-found relatives in the State of Maine. Her illness had made her anxious to visit them, and although we were not yet able to afford the expense of so costly a trip, her happiness was our greatest concern, and we acquiesced in her wishes. This pinched us so closely for money that my land was sold for taxes. But crops, despite the chinch-bugs, were good, and when my corn and rye were sold, our crop of native hay harvested, the splendid potatoes dug, the sorghum worked up on the shares, we were far from being unprepared for winter.

I had decided to try another experiment in wintering stock; so I took for a man named Frank Mecker, ten head of cattle to feed until spring. It was a wet winter. Toward spring the cattle tramped mud-holes near the creek, and would sometimes get into places from which it took much effort to extricate them. I lost three head of stock, and Mr. Mecker one, in this way. Insisting that his stock was registered, and that, despite the work I had done to bring his cattle safely through the winter, the loss of this one was my fault, I had to lose the pay for all of them. Thus, Kansas cattle involved me as deeply as did those from Texas.

In February, I went to Council Grove on business. I was to pay some debts, get some goods and return that day; but on the way I noticed that the Neosho river near the old Mission — as we called the Indian school-house — was nearly to the wagon-bed, and I hastened home as rapidly as possible for fear of being delayed in crossing. Only two hours had elapsed since I crossed it in safety, but the water had risen very perceptibly when I again reached the river. Still I did not think it unsafe, and drove into the stream. In the midst of the rapidly swelling current, a sudden swirl of drifting débris struck my wagon and forced me several yards down the flood. The ponies could swim, and I was not much alarmed until the tongue of the wagon caught in a stout sapling. I climbed out to loosen it, and the current forced the wagon-bed away and left me dancing upon the running-gear. The box was gone, so I devoted myself to saving the horses. The traces were soon loosened, and with a lunge or two the animals safely reached the shore nearest home. Just as the horses started, the hind wheels of the wagon were rapidly turned over, and, lying upon my back on the water, I saw a wheel coming straight at my devoted head. With all my strength, I raised myself, and intercepted the blow by catching the wheel with my boot. I was only a few minutes after the wheel passed in gaining the shore I had just left, but by this time my bath made me feel as if I would enjoy a little friction and a Turkish towel. It was worse than a cold shower-bath in winter to wear my dripping garments, and it was with much comfort, after walking a mile to Reverend William Bradford's house, that I donned some ministerial garments. It was the first time I had worn them since the days of my boyish efforts in the new chapels of England, and I would never have believed they could again be so comfortable. My own clothes resented this partiality. They had shared my immersion, and now they really "froze" to me despite my frantic efforts to discard them.

Kind friends cared for my horses, and kind friends took me across at a safer crossing. I rode one of the half-drowned ponies home, and found my family mourning me as dead, having heard that the horses had reached the bank without me, and that I was lost in the stream.

In the spring of 1872, by having ten acres of sod broken on my farm, I found my land under cultivation to amount to sixty acres. Having learned the advantages of crop rotation, I decided to put my last year's corn land and the new ten acres in spring wheat. When the stout double-shovels had shoveled in the wheat, I planted ten acres of oats. By June of that year, all of the minor crops were planted, and I had sixty acres of as promising prospects for grain and other products as one need wish to see.

But the seasons of Kansas are always springing new surprises upon the people, especially the farmers of the State. There was much rain that year, and although crops were good, many lost much produce from the sudden and constant rainfall. Often our large log house was full of persons who could not cross the stream until the waters subsided.

A sad calamity occurred that May, at the selfsame spot where I came near being drowned. A young married couple named Somers, a gentleman named Roberts, and the beautiful and accomplished daughter of Judge Huffaker — Miss Laura — attempted to cross this stream when the current was very swift. In sight of the old Mission where her father had taught the careless Kaws, Miss Huffaker and her friends were caught in the swelling flood of the Neosho river, buried under the overturned carriage and horses, and drowned. So well known as the friend of the Indian, and the representative of good government, was Judge Huffaker, that not only Morris county, but the State of Kansas, sympathized with him in his sad affliction. Over the recovered bodies the people for miles around Council Grove gathered and dropped tears of regret and sympathy. The main streams of Kansas were then bridged, but the smaller ones were often dangerous, and the pioneers of Kansas incurred much danger and hardship in crossing these narrow, deep creeks and rivers, which filled so rapidly one could hardly tell whether or not it was safe to enter them.

I had always been greatly interested in the education of the youth of the State, and at this time and for several subsequent years I served as clerk of our school district in Neosho township, Morris county, Kansas. Some of the most pleasant memories of my life cluster around the educational work. I well remember Isaac T. Goodnow, the State Superintendent from the year 1861 until 1864. During the first year of his work, he traveled over the sparsely-settled State by team, visiting its every settled county. Dr. McVicar, another Superintendent, was also a valued friend, and one to whom the youth of Kansas owe much gratitude for the splendid work he did for the schools of the State.

My experience as a farmer that year, despite the losses from wet weather, was very satisfactory. Oats made fifty, wheat thirty and corn seventy-five bushels to the acre. Millet, buckwheat, potatoes and other crops did well; and when everything was marketed, I paid off six hundred dollars of the indebtedness on my farm. In the following spring, I was also able to redeem my land, the aggregate delinquent tax on which amounted to two hundred and five dollars, and to pay off a mortgage and its interest of four hundred and seventy-five dollars. The lifting of these debts removed a heavy load from our minds, and made us feel for the first time that prosperity had at last paid us a visit.

My millet, hay and wheat were harvested and my corn was too far along for us to fear mishaps, when one day I called to my wife:

"Lottie, come and look at that queer cloud!"

She came to the door.

"It is a cloud of grasshoppers," she answered. "See! they are drifting down like green flakes."

Sure enough! they were beginning to settle. As they came nearer the ground, they darkened the sky like a storm-cloud, and made a noise like distant thunder. A little later, they were organized into a devastating army, destroying every living thing tender enough for mastication within reach of their voracious jaws. The grasshoppers were more indefatigable than the sappers and miners during a siege, or the soldiers in the open battle-field. They worked without cessation. I went out late at night and put my ear to a stalk of tall corn. I could hear them gnawing away in the darkness, and grieving, I suppose, that owing to the hardness of the grain they could only eat the husk. When they had eaten up everything else, they went leisurely to work and consumed the winter wheat, after which they deposited their eggs in the ground, and went into winter quarters ready for developments in the spring.

Talk of the encroachment of a Napoleon Bonaparte! The French army was a small affair compared with the legions that invaded Kansas in 1873. If we could only have imitated the Russians and destroyed our Moscows before these savage troops quartered in our Kremlins, it would have been more satisfactory. Abundant rains fell that fall, and in the overflowing of rivers and creeks, the eggs, from which reinforcements had been expected by the advance army of grasshoppers, were swept away.

An event of interest to the entire State in general and to Morris county in particular, occurred in 1873. The Kaw or Kansas Indians, our native tribe, were removed from the State. The Government of the United States had long promised to send them to a reservation in the Indian Territory, but so far had failed to do so. There were only about two hundred of this once large tribe left, and there was very little sentiment wasted upon them when they bade farewell to their long-time home, and left Kansas for good.

The summer of 1874 was a trying time for Kansans. A scorching drouth visited the State. Crops were almost totally destroyed, and in the autumn the grasshoppers again paid us a visit. Everything left was destroyed by them. They seemed to really enjoy onions, and when, to save my cabbage, I used large quantities of salt, their relish for that esculent seemed greatly increased. They even ate the stumps of the cabbage-stalks into the ground. Kansas grasshoppers were as well posted on relishes as those of Minnesota.

Christmas Day once more approached, and my wife suggested that we make use of our losses by eating one of the fat turkeys which had become enormous in size from the quantities of grasshoppers it had devoured. So a turkey dinner was prepared, and despite pests, drouth, and failure, we gathered with some dear friends around a board laden with the good cheer no one knew better how to prepare than Mrs. Brake. Prayers were read, and we made it a real anniversary day. Thank God for Christmas and its blessedness! Thank Him, too, for the Christ it commemorates, the Saviour who though our "sins are as scarlet makes them like snow," and whose mercies are numberless. Yea, thank God — the Giver and Taker — the Creator of the material and the spiritual worlds, the great Sharer of all our joys and the Comforter of all our sorrows.

The winter passed rapidly away, and the spring of 1875 approached. There was much snow, and everything gave promise of an early and a fruitful season. The farmers of Kansas began with good heart to prepare for planting their crops. Should the precious seed fail this year to reach fruition, starvation doubtless stared many in the face. There was much distress in the State, and in the parts where the most damage had been done, meetings were held, and aid was solicited for the sufferers. Several of these meetings were held in Council Grove. Committees were selected to secure aid from the East by writing to friends, and giving them a description of the poverty and suffering among certain families in that part of the State. Many volunteered everywhere to do this work, and the result was that barrels of provisions, boxes of clothing and hundreds of dollars in money were sent into Kansas for the relief of the needy. But while the hearts of thousands were opened to the wants of the drouth sufferers, that some were indifferent or doubtful of their needs will be shown by the following letter:

"THORNDYKE STATION, MAINE, March 26, 1875.

"*Dear Brother and Sister Brake:* We were pleased to receive your favor of the 16th inst. Epistolary correspondence, even among strangers, has a tendency to draw into a closer relationship even people of different nationalities. In perusing your letter and thinking over the suffering of men and animals, the great waste of property, the exorbitant prices charged for freight to the sufferers, almost paralyze belief in the fatherhood of God and the brotherhood of man.

"I am in my seventieth year, and cannot do much by way of business. Am not now able to help contribute to Kansas relief. But I tried to get up a fund for seed wheat for your community, and when I mentioned it people said it was visionary to get up a donation party for people three thousand miles away. I can only talk the matter up, hoping that Kansas will soon emerge from her trouble.

"For the present, farewell. THOMAS B. HUSSEY.
LIZZIE K. HUSSEY."

It was pleasant to me to be able to refuse the aid offered me, and see it given to those needing it worse than ourselves. I had seed wheat on hand, and early began to get my land planted in wheat, corn, and other crops. My sheep did well that year; some of the fleeces weighed twelve to fourteen pounds. The weather was so hot that summer that two of my men fainted and had to be carried out of the harvest-field. One night, when our day's work in the field was done, we sat up rather late, the women chatting in the house and the men smoking outside the door. Later, we all went to bed, my wife and daughter and a lady friend up stairs, and the men below.

About daylight I was awakened by a rippling, gurgling sound, and, rising up in bed, I saw water running under the door and across the room. Upon opening the door, the water rushed in and soon rose ankle-deep. I called the harvesters, but they did not get up. "Do you want to be drowned?" I shouted, for I did not know how deep it might get; "if you do, stay where you are."

"We thought you were getting us out a little too early," said one of the men, as they all sprang from the beds. "We'll get up, you bet!"

In ten minutes the water, still rising, was a foot deep in the house. The women stayed up stairs, but Lizzie ran down and gathered some of her chickens into barrels. I found my swine enjoying a good boat-ride. They were swimming about in their big troughs, and when the pens were pulled down, and they were allowed to seek refuge wherever they could find it, they took to the water as naturally as ducks. A view from the top of the house showed an expanse of water over three miles in circumference. The streams which had caused the overflow were evidently still rising, and my shocks of wheat by scores were deserting the field. Fences, wood and other loose property were keeping them company, and the sun was shining as serenely on the muddy waters of the landscape as if nothing had happened.

We had no fire; there was a foot of water in the fireplace; so we breakfasted on bread and bacon, eggs and milk, and by way of variety again "viewed the landscape o'er." My wife kept her eyes fixed on a log near the house, and, after two hours' watching, reported the water as falling. By noon we could get out of the house.

Hot, dry weather set in, and by the assistance of hired hands and neighbors, I saved most of my wheat. When threshed it brought three hundred dollars.

On the whole, Morris county was redeemed. The abundant rains, the well-soaked soil, made the crops develop rapidly, and as the weather was dry in October and November, they were well garnered.

The weather in the winter of 1875-6 was cold, for Kansas, the thermometer often registering ten degrees below zero; but to myself, who had often been out in Minnesota weather when it was forty and fifty degrees below zero, it did not seem so very cold. I had planted ten acres of rye and fifteen of winter wheat, and had increased my tillable land to seventy acres.

The next spring I secured a corn-planter, and soon had my corn planted. A little later the millet was sown, harrowed, and rolled. In July we had several heavy rainstorms, and all the streams were badly swollen. The one near our home was too high to be safely crossed, and for three days and nights a minister named Dearborn was entertained in our home, until the waters were no longer in a dangerous condition and could be crossed in safety. Ministers who preached Christ's gospel, physicians who healed the sick, teachers who taught the children, all, as Kansans, had a serious time in fulfilling their duties, even as late as 1876.

It was astonishing, however, the small amount of damage done by the floods. The corn would bend, and some of the small grain would be carried away, but the weight of the remaining grain would compensate for the loss, and the corn would ripen just as well. Millions of chinchbugs drank themselves to death, too, in the floods, and were spared the trouble of devouring the crops. Dry weather had to be awaited for the sowing of millet and other late crops, but the extra yield more than compensated for the delay. Even prairie hay needs to be allowed to seed the ground and strengthen the roots, a necessity few observe, and the wet season gave the grass an opportunity to do this, so that the future yield was greatly increased.

In October, 1876, our daughter, who had been visiting friends in the East for ten months, returned to her Kansas home. She had made the journey alone with true Kansas pluck, and on the return trip had stopped in Philadelphia, and visited the great Centennial exhibition. We were so overjoyed to have her with us after her long absence that the labors of harvest seemed wonderfully lightened by the thought that at any time we could look into her pleasant face, and listen to her cheery voice.

By our usual anniversary day, the work for the year was done. On the farm, corn had yielded forty bushels to the acre, wheat twenty, rye twenty-five. Other crops, except millet, were fair, and we had the finest animals in the fattening-pen that I had ever seen. So we had an abundant supply of hams for winter use, with enough for sale to buy our clothing for a year. At the beginning of the new year, although we had no boys, and must depend entirely upon hired help for assistance, though failure of crops, grasshoppers and many other calamities had visited us, yet with other Kansans, our heads were above water, our debts were decreasing, and our health as a family was excellent. Yet, as I have attempted to show, the early Kansas farmer, who broke out the soil, and turned the prairie into tillable and tilled land, had no easy task. We could afford to buy little machinery, and the unceasing toil and effort told on us as the years stole by; but, with hundreds of other Kansas farmers, I found that agriculture paid, and that the careful, honest, painstaking tiller of the soil need never give a note which when due he would be unable to honor.

January, 1877, was a hard, snowy time, but February was one of the most delightful months a Kansas winter has produced. In March, on the 15th, occurred the wedding of our only child. In the log cabin where she had passed her happy youth, a Christian minister named Reverend T. Hutton joined her hand with that of Newton E. Fisher, and pronounced the sacred words that made them husband and wife. When the supper her loving mother had prepared was over, we bade our darling farewell. She would not be far from us, but to say that we missed this girl who had been the crowning blessing of our lives, would feebly express our feelings. We vaguely felt that although happily and prosperously married to the son of our early benefactor, yet she could never be quite the same to us as before her marriage.

Ah! we cannot see into the future. The time came afterwards, when I was a stricken, widowed, childless mourner, that Lizzie, then a widow with two lovely children, came back to me to be the stay of my declining years. I cannot even think what life would be without the happy faces and merry voices of my daughter's children.

The year 1877 was a splendid one for Kansas. Abundant crops were raised, and people who had judged the State by the drouth of 1860, or the barrenness of 1874, were now changing their opinion. Immigration into Kansas was rapid, and school-houses, churches and beautiful homes were increasing by hundreds and thousands. Railroads were spreading like a network over the State, and the persons who had most striven in behalf of success — the farmers of Kansas — now felt themselves upon the highway to prosperity. As to Morris county, the removal of the Kaw Indians, and the placing of their lands upon the market, had materially added to the development of her latent resources of soil and climate. That delightful summer, free from floods, drouth, or pests, will always be a pleasant Kansas memory, and the busy scenes presented on almost every farm, when new bins and granaries had to be built for the abundant crops, will never be forgotten.

Time rolled away so swiftly that Christmas was upon us ere we knew it. We were saddened as we thought of the fact that we were alone. My dear wife and myself were thousands of miles away from every living relative, and our adopted daughter was no longer beside our hearth. But we were not forgotten. First there came a letter from Lottie's dear English sister, breathing a message of good-will from the land of our youth for the land of our adoption, as well as sweet words of Christmas congratulation for ourselves. Then there came a merry party of young folks, including our beloved Lizzie and her husband, to spend the evening with us. We forgot our loneliness, and I heaped the old chimney with logs so often that half a cord of sturdy oak was consumed ere the gay revelers left us. It mattered not that the mistletoe was missing. Under the quaint rafters of the old farm-house the young folks played merry games, and enjoyed the kissing quite as well when in mock marriages they performed osculatory feats by way of ratification. They danced, too. The music did not accord very well with the time kept by the tripping feet of lads and lassies, as it used to in old London, but in the absence of a parlor organ, a good-natured fellow *whistled* the tunes, and Lottie and I enjoyed the performance more than any other couple present. Kansas people do not need the environments of fashion to aid in telling the "old, old story," nor in spending an evening of pure, unalloyed enjoyment.

After long years of toil at farming I decided to rent my land out during the year 1878, and fill a contract I had taken to supply a brick manufacturer with a hundred cords of wood. Accordingly, I rented my farm on the shares to two brothers named Johnson, who, by delaying their corn-planting for rain until too late, raised nothing.

The next year, I rented my farm to a widow who expected to buy it when she received a pension for her dead husband's service as a soldier. She gave up the place in a short time, and I leased it for three years to a man named Simmonds, for half the peach and one-third of all other crops. Mr. Simmonds soon sold out to a Mr. Dent. Peaches were of a great size that year, and were very plentiful. My orchard yielded over five hundred bushels.

By March, 1879, my wood was delivered, and the four hundred dollars received for it left a profit of two hundred dollars over the expense of the work.

I now had one of the most productive bottom farms in this part of Kansas, and many persons sought to rent the land each year. The remainder of the uplands of the Kaw reserve was now on the market, and I purchased eighty acres of it, and added the same to my farm. It requires time to secure the right to Government lands, and I did not receive the patent (signed by President Cleveland) until 1885. But I was now the owner of two hundred and forty acres of very rich land.

Despite the stringent terms concerning Government lands, many clever persons secured farms at little trouble and expense. In place of houses, some put up two crotches about twenty feet apart, and extended a long pole from one to the other. Up to this "ridgepole," as they called it, on either side boards were slanted at an angle of some forty-five degrees, and boards were also put at the end. The "living" done in such houses consisted of putting a fire on the ground over which coffee was boiled. With cold victuals to accompany the coffee, an occasional meal was taken in these elegant new homes.

Upon the witness's testimony depended much; he always asserted that a good frame house of a certain size had been built upon the claim. When I learned the requirements, I set to work and put up a good log building upon my Kaw purchase. During the same time I built a good frame house upon my farm, and my wife and I moved into it, leaving a tenant in our old one. It cost us an effort to leave the dear old dwelling where we had experienced the joys and sorrows of Kansas life since 1867, and which stood upon the site of the shanty occupied by pioneers most of the time since 1861; but our new home was comfortable, and we were soon content with our location. We had long contemplated building, and it was pleasant to think that every part of our house, even to the weather-boarding and shingles, was made from our native timber.

Corn made forty bushels to the acre in 1880, and all of my renters did well for themselves and for us.

For the year 1881, I let the farm to an enterprising bachelor named Crowley, who kept bachelor's hall in the old log house. Excellent results followed his efforts at farming, and I gave him possession of my new home and moved with my wife to the house now ready on the Kaw land.

A well was dug, a pasture fenced, trees set out, and a garden was planted with vegetables and flowers. We soon found ourselves at home on the sunny hillside, and greatly relieved by having the responsibility of the larger farm off our hands. About this time, a man named Collier bought one of my eighties for fifteen hundred dollars.

There was a mortgage on the whole quarter-section, and he agreed to pay it off as part of the price paid for the land. So at last we were practically free from debt, and could enjoy life without adversity constantly staring us in the face.

Having five hundred dollars on hand, I decided to add to our claim dwelling two comfortable rooms. My wife willingly acquiesced in the plan, and in two months we had two nice rooms, plastered, painted, papered, and carpeted. I papered the parlor, and as it was my first attempt in that line, so I declared it should be the last. If the sisters like "Samantha" want to climb on barrels and boxes to paper ceilings, I have no objections, but I said solemnly to Lottie as I finished the job:

"No more o' that an' thou lovest me!"

By 1884, we had a beautiful home, with trees, shrubs, vines and flowers in abundance, a never-failing well of good water, twenty acres of land under cultivation, and everything about us showing that the blight of debt rested no longer upon our efforts. Our garden was a great pleasure to both of us. Every variety of vegetable was grown, and few visited us that did not find something that would tempt the appetite. Besides the common vegetables, of which we always raised many, we were fond of planting mushrooms, egg-plant, vegetable oysters, the Jerusalem artichoke, the truffle of France, cauliflowers, and celery. Some of our friends insisted that these things in the vegetable world corresponded to eels, frogs and turtles in the animal world, and with them were not fit to eat. But under the witching influence of Charlotte's dainty cookery, they always changed their minds.

I was now seventy years old, but with a double-shovel

plow I put in four acres of oats, plowed the ground and planted twenty acres of corn. The care of the garden, except Mrs. Brake's flowers, of course devolved upon me. I also had four cows to milk, for, although an excellent dairy woman, Lottie would never milk a cow. There were two things Lizzie had always done better than her mother — milk cows and ride horses.

But we were aging, and I decided now to give up farming and remove to Council Grove, where I had built us a house. So, when Providence seemed to favor our wishes and a man offered three thousand five hundred dollars for the farm, I accepted his offer. In October, the man gave me fifteen hundred dollars cash, and two notes of a thousand dollars each, bearing eight per cent. interest. One of these notes was paid in money and labor at the end of four years, and the other, though due in two, was not paid for eight years; and then it was settled in a court of law, where I lost over four hundred dollars.

The crops did not pass with the land, and I did not have to give possession until March 1, 1885, at which time I was to receive my Kaw land patent. There were no mortgages, taxes or other debts to settle, and we had plenty of leisure to get ready for our new residence. Looking forward to this time, I had built two nice houses in Council Grove, and as one of them was unoccupied, in November, 1884, I built a kitchen to it, had it cleaned and papered, and on the 25th of the month we moved into the house, where to-day I am writing the simple story of my life.

CHAPTER XIV.

OUR EXPERIENCE IN COUNCIL GROVE.

As my principal and interest came in, I laid the money out in improvements in Council Grove. The long years spent in Morris county, the many warm friends about us, and our unwillingness to form new ties at our ages, would have made it impossible for us to invest in property in any other Kansas town but Council Grove. In 1886, I built a third residence, and my now widowed daughter left her large farm to tenants, and came with her children to reside in the new cottage.

New houses were then being built in Council Grove, and a building society flourished like a sunflower in Kansas soil. I built two residences, each costing a thousand dollars, and rented them for ten and twelve dollars per month. My property now consisted of five neat cottages, a block each away from our two railroads—the Missouri, Kansas & Texas, and the Missouri Pacific. I again built another cottage for five hundred dollars, and up to the crisis of 1893, the rents of these residences provided for all of our wants. After putting some improvements upon my houses in order to make the tenants comfortable, I invested my surplus cash in fruit trees and vines. I never expected to live to enjoy their fruitage, but I believe that the man who plants a tree is to some extent a public benefactor, and I took the greatest pains with my new investment. I am happy to say that I have lived to enjoy an abundance of grapes and cherries from that planting, and the vineyards and trees have not yet reached full maturity.

Grief came to me in her saddest form in the year 1891, for I could not blind my eyes to the fact that the time when I must be separated from my lifelong companion was near at hand. She was taken down with *la grippe*, and from this time rapidly failed in health and spirits. Partial paralysis made it impossible for her to walk, and I carried her in my arms like a child. Her patience, fortitude and unfailing kindness made her more beloved than ever, and her care the solace and comfort of my saddened life. Toward the close her heart sometimes ceased to beat, and once she lay unconscious for many hours. Then she would rally and seem better for days. On January 18, 1893, I carried her into the dining-room for the last time. In the dusk of the evening, her physicians — Doctors Bradford and Crawford — were hastily summoned; my wife, my brave, true darling, was dying! After hours of unconsciousness, she recovered, and spoke in her old sweet tones, asking for Charlie — her grandson. After her voice failed, her eyes seemed to brighten. She motioned for me to sit where she could look into my face, and seemed perfectly conscious until the last. On the morning of January 20, in the arms of her loving daughter, with her eyes fixed upon my face, one of the purest of mortal spirits passed from earth to be with the one Lord and His Father in whom she implicitly trusted. Her last words to me were:

> "May thy life, from errors free,
> Be a long bright day to thee;
> And at last, when wearied grown
> Of the joys which thou hast known,
> And thy spirit sinks to rest,
> May angels guard thee to the blest,
> Where we'll meet forevermore,
> Freed from all the toils of yore."

January 22, 1893, her dear remains were laid to rest in Greenwood cemetery, Morris county, Kansas.

What better evidence can we have of a higher life than the calmness with which the good embrace death? Once a soul is knit to that invisible world by the strong tie of an affection which bridges the gulf separating this life and the life beyond, nothing can shake the faith of the one who waits in the immortality enjoyed by the one who watches. The certainty of our spiritual nature, the longing for its full development, the knowledge that it can only be so developed by immortality, intensifies our faith, our love, our hope, into a climax that only culminates when the angel of death releases us from a world of which we are long-time weary. Ah, Lottie! the forty-seven years spent together on this earth are mere points of time in the great circle of eternity which we shall together enjoy when you come to escort me to the life beyond the stars.

As I write these words, my heart thrills with gratitude at the thought that although sometimes I have fallen into unbelief or have grown lukewarm in the cause of my Master, yet He has spared me at this great age to testify to His goodness and mercy toward men and nations. Amidst all the griefs, the trials and conflicts of this life, I have never doubted but that the time would come when the knowledge of Jesus Christ would cover the earth "as the waters shall cover the sea." As to the certainty of an Infinite Creator, an acquaintance with many different Indian tribes has convinced me that the lowest creature recognizes the truth of His existence and power. I am persuaded from a study of man, especially of my own heart, that there is a law governing man, as well as nature, and that if this be true, this law or first cause which man calls God also governs the soul or what is best in man.

If this be true, we could never understand Him without some one to reveal Him to us. This revelation, His divine Son Jesus Christ has made. Were we not a part of the Creator's nature and attributes, we would not have been worthy of such a sacrifice as was offered upon Calvary. I rejoice in the Sonship of Christ, who as my brother lifts me to an heirship with Him, and thus makes possible a future meeting with my beloved.

One who has failed to experience a similar trial cannot understand the loneliness of solitude unshared for the first time in life. But kind friends helped me to bear the burdens of this time, nursed me back to health when I gave way to a protracted illness, and after awhile I could stand up once more and look the world in the face.

When I found myself entirely alone, I devoted my time to opening up a correspondence with my English relatives. My own communications, as well as those of my brothers and sisters, had miscarried so often that we had finally lost a knowledge of each other's whereabouts. A card to a cousin at Sherborne, Dorset county, England, brought me an answer concerning many members of my family. I was surprised to learn that I had over fifty near relatives still living in England. But still more surprised that these were all on one side of the family, and that of my grandfather's family the only descendants left were four cousins and myself. I attribute my advantage in longevity over my relatives to the activity of my nature and the constant change incident to a pioneer's life.

Many invitations to visit England reached me, and I fully purposed going, when I was stricken down with *la grippe*, and that highly fashionable disease unfitted me for an ocean voyage. Then came the crisis of 1893, and so impossible was it to collect indebtedness, rents, or interest, that I was compelled for the time to abandon the trip to Europe. I had hoped, for my daughter's sake, to learn something of the piece of land deeded to our family by the benevolent Earl Digby, but failed to do so.

Through all the years since leaving Topeka, I had not united with any church. I was no bigot, and really enjoyed every form of worship; yet the beautiful ritual of the Episcopal church had been my ideal, and we were too few in number to have a church of that denomination in Council Grove. But, believing it my duty to be connected with some individual church, I decided to identify myself with the one in which I was baptized as an infant, and to which my parents then belonged — the Congregational church. I did so, and am still a member of that society.

In May, 1894, the Ministerial Union was held in Emporia, Kansas, and, with many others interested in Christian work, I visited the city and attended the meetings. I had seen Emporia in 1861; it was then only a village, lately planned and laid out by Preston B. Plumb — afterwards United States Senator from Kansas. Thirty-three years had made a great change in Senator Plumb's city. As I drove over it in a friend's carriage, I saw the spires of between twenty and thirty churches; school-houses of beautiful and modern design, hundreds of magnificent homes, a splendid college building, and the State Normal School. This school is justly the pride of the State, and with its two sisters — the Agricultural College at Manhattan and the State University at Lawrence — forms one of the grandest systems for higher education possible to any State.

President A. R. Taylor, that "prince of educators," was, and still is, at the head of this institution; his pupils numbered over thirteen hundred, and since then the number has increased to almost fifteen hundred. Long may this noble, Christian gentleman remain at the head of the Normal work for teachers in this great State.

In this visit I met a gentleman from Wabaunsee who was born in Sherborne, England, and we had a very pleasant chat together.

I had not been able to visit great meetings very often, and this one so filled me with enthusiasm that I decided to accept the invitation to attend the Kansas Christian Endeavor Convention, in May of the same year. I had a curiosity, too, to see the Capital City, which I had not visited since 1863. So I accepted Honorable T. F. Doran's invitation of hospitality, and spent a few days in his Topeka home. My granddaughter — Laura — was a delegate to the convention from the Christian church in Council Grove, and of course, with her mother, accompanied me. Through Mr. Doran's kindness, we visited the Kansas capitol building, the churches, colleges, asylums, and many other interesting places.

When I took my family to Topeka in 1863, in order that my daughter might have a year in college, the place could hardly have been called a city. Now, as the electric cars whirled us about under the electric lights, and glancing from the wide, paved avenues and streets to the splendid hotels, homes and public buildings, I took in the full significance of the fact that I was in a great modern city; I was lost in astonishment. My mind went back to the time when I could well remember that not even railroads were in existence. Modern progress is indeed remarkable.

Perhaps nothing was to me so enjoyable as the renewal of acquaintance with my old friend, Dr. Peter McVicar, President of Washburn College. During the long years since 1864, I had not seen him. When the excellent lecture he gave before the Endeavorers was over, I visited him at his house, and presented him with some files of his educational journal sent to me when I was a district clerk in Morris county and he was State Superintendent of Public Instruction. Our mutual pleasure may be imagined at thus being spared in old age to renew our former acquaintance.

Holbrook Hall, the Washburn College library, greatly interested me. Both sexes are admitted to the reading-rooms, and there is provided a well-arranged library of six thousand volumes, with the leading periodicals, free to all visitors.

My daughter was anxious to find her school building of 1863, and after much inquiry learned that it was now the residence of Bishop Thomas, of the Protestant Episcopal diocese. We also found our old home — now badly shaken and decayed — and Lizzie was delighted to find the tree where she had hidden her bonnet during the Quantrell raid scare in 1863. What she then supposed the guerrilla leader would want with a little girl's bonnet, is beyond my comprehension.

In 1894, occurred the great railroad strike. The American Railway Union entered into a sympathetic strike against the Pullman Palace Car Company of Chicago, and the terrible results of this strike are beyond comprehension. With the commerce of the country "tied," hundreds out of employment, and the suffering to both capitalists and laborers extreme, there followed a severe drouth, and the most terrible hot winds known in Kansas and the west for years.

In four days' time the scorching blast had destroyed the prospects for crops, and the fate of the strike sufferers was sealed. Products would be higher than ever, money still as scarce, and all classes would have to bear their part of the calamity. Farmers raised but little; for example, one farmer who had planted one hundred and twenty-five acres raised no ears of corn whatever upon the stalks of fodder, and the latter was of very poor quality.

The year 1895 partially atoned for the poor crops of the previous year, and prosperity is beginning once more to smile upon Kansas. Morris county has suffered in common with all of the other counties of the State, but she is emerging from her distress, and peace and prosperity are holding out to her rich promises of future success.

In 1861, when I first settled in Kansas, nearly every person was sick. Distress was common, and constant toil and effort were necessary to sustain life. The climate told on every person, and many became discouraged and abandoned their pioneer homes. As years went by, destructive prairie fires, which often destroyed miles of fencing and tons of precious hay, swept over the country. We were not safe from this evil for years, although the herd law, which prevented the turning out of stock, helped mitigate its effects by doing away with fences. Grasshoppers, drouths, storms, war, have all visited Kansas, and in them Morris county has borne her share; but I have lived to see thrift and courage conquer all obstacles, the climate become healthful, and our beautiful prairies teeming with thousands of cultured people living in homes of beauty and comfort.

Council Grove, the capital of Morris county, although not exhibiting the marked growth of many Kansas towns, has nothing in her development for which her citizens need blush.

In 1859, when I first saw this settlement far out upon the "desert," Indians, cowboys and traders were its visitors, only a few daring men its actual settlers, and the prospects for its future entirely dependent upon its usefulness to the Santa Fé trail and trade. In 1861, when I saw the place again, it was yet a mere village. The mail service still started for the west from this point; however, a store and hotel and several other buildings gave promise of future growth, and the town was yet a rendezvous for traders and travelers who were crossing the plains. Junction City and Emporia soon rivaled Council Grove, the first securing the mail service, the second the Santa Fé Railroad.

Despite all this, the town has grown with a steady, permanent growth. Well-to-do farmers and stock-raisers surround it, and energetic, honorable people dwell within it. Saloons are as far away from Council Grove, it is to be hoped, as the eastern State line, and the youth of the city have every advantage in school and church facilities. Six denominations — Congregational, Presbyterian, Christian, Methodist, Southern Methodist, and Baptist — hold services each Sunday, and over six hundred school children are gathered in our city school-rooms under the care of excellent teachers. A good high school and library add to the interest and usefulness of the educational work in Council Grove.

The Missouri Pacific Railroad has a good round-house in the town, and the Missouri, Kansas & Texas has a new, well-built and commodious depot. The pay-roll of these two roads in Council Grove is about ten thousand dollars per month. Good mills and an elevator furnish employment to many men. An elegant opera house, imposing bank buildings, halls for all of the benevolent societies, grace the city, and hundreds of pleasant homes, surrounded with beautiful lawns fragrant each summer with vines and shrubbery, testify to the beauty-loving spirit of the citizens.

One of the oldest and fairest of Kansas towns, Council Grove has before her a future whose prosperity can only exceed the interest of her history in the past.

CHAPTER XV.

CONCLUSION.

As I come to the concluding chapter of my long life, it may be asked what is my political belief? I cannot reply without mentioning the differences of opinion concerning political rights between this country and England, my native land, where a property qualification is necessary. When I left Great Britain, in 1847, I had never owned property enough to allow me the privilege of voting, or in any way helping to control or influence the laws by which I was governed. My interest in politics consisted in loyalty to the gracious Victoria and love for our common realm. I was entirely ignorant of many of the laws of the land, and felt little inclination to investigate them. In 1851, when I became the owner of thirteen acres of land on Long Island, I decided it was time to take an interest in the politics of my adopted country. I was so entirely ignorant that I was surprised to learn that I must take out papers declaring my intention to become a citizen of the United States, forswear my allegiance to my sovereign, and take oath to support the Constitution of the United States.

I first voted in Minnesota, and as I had made no study of the subject, I voted as a sleek-tongued politician near me advised — for James Buchanan. The death of President Lincoln first roused me to examine the principles of the political parties about me, and after careful examination and mature deliberation, I came to the conclusion that the Republican party advocated the principles in which Americans should believe, and from that time to the present have voted the Republican ticket.

My experience in this matter has forced me to the conviction that foreigners need to be educated as well as to be shaken loose from their old-world ideas of politics, before they should vote in this country. An Englishman coming to America who never had voted, living here several years without political privilege, my vote was at once eagerly sought when slavery hung in the balance. I was very angry, too, when some persons challenged my first vote. I said:

"I am entitled to more respect than you, for I have adopted this Government from choice, while you were born here and are Americans from necessity."

But I lived to see the time when I was glad that the friends of the negro challenged my vote. I have been staunch to my adopted land, and have truly learned to love her better than the land of my birth, for I am, and have been for years, in favor of the protection of American industries and American interests.

The rights of Americans as contrasted with those of Englishmen are striking. Not only can a man vote in the United States, thus helping to make the laws, but he can hold office without being a property-holder. Poverty cannot grind him into political serfdom. In England, the opposite is true.

Again, in America men are not imprisoned for debt; while in England, even when "whitewashed"— as freeing a man from debt is there called — when he leaves the walls of the "whitewashing" establishment and seeks a home in new lands, where he stands some opportunity of beginning life under more favorable circumstances, he is liable to arrest. I once sent money for passage across the Atlantic to a relative who had unfortunately a small debt against him. His ship was stopped by officers with a search warrant; the cry of "thief" sounded through the ship, and the man was taken like a malefactor from his friends, forced into the officers' boat, and, heavily ironed, carried to Portsmouth and lodged in jail.

For myself, the past has gone, never to return. Age will soon prevent me from taking part in the affairs of county or State. But even as I rejoice in the knowledge of many superior advantages possessed by this country over my native land, my constant prayer is that these United States may never fall into the condition of low wages and poor living which characterize the United Kingdom. If times seem dull in America, recent letters from England assure me that it is worse there, and that the condition of affairs facing English laborers is truly appalling.

Many have been the changes since I first opened my eyes to the light in my old English home. Steam and electricity have done wonders for the material world. Man has developed as a spiritual being. The Gospel of Christ has reached even the far-off heathen isles. The chains of slavery have been flung off by every civilized nation. The principles of purity and peace are being promulgated. Armenia has awakened the slumbering sympathy of humanity. Cuba is throwing off her chains. The twentieth century will witness an awakened humanity, a new era of world-wide peace and prosperity. May America and England — the two great nations that are united by a common language and religion — recognize not only the Edisons and Tyndalls, the Lincolns and Gladstones who have aided in this work, but the hearts of the common people on each side of the Atlantic.

t